P9-EMH-875

The Good Shepherd

ALSO BY MORDECAI SIEGAL
AND MATTHEW MARGOLIS

*The Golden Years: A Pet Owner's Guide
to the Golden Retriever*

Woof!

When Good Dogs Do Bad Things

I Just Got a Puppy: What Do I Do?

Underdog

Good Dog, Bad Dog

BY MORDECAI SIEGAL

Cornell Book of Cats

UC/Davis Book of Horses

UC/Davis Book of Dogs

*Choosing the Perfect Dog for You and
Your Family*

Understanding the Dog You Love

Understanding the Cat You Love

Happy Kittens, Happy Cats

Your New Best Friend

Happy Dog/Happy Owner

A Dog for the Kids

The Simon & Schuster Guide to Cats

The Good Cat Book

The Good Dog Book

*The Mordecai Siegal Happy Pet/Happy
Owner Book*

BY MATTHEW MARGOLIS

The Dog in Your Life (with Catherine
Swan)

*Some Swell Pup: Or Are You Sure You
Want a Dog?* (with Maurice
Sendak)

The Liberated Dog

The Good Shepherd

A Pet Owner's Guide to the German Shepherd Dog

BY

MORDECAI SIEGAL

and

MATTHEW MARGOLIS

Photographs by

Barbara von Hoffmann

LITTLE, BROWN AND COMPANY Boston New York Toronto London

Copyright © 1996 by Mordecai Siegal and Matthew Margolis

All rights reserved. No part of this book may be reproduced in any form or by any electronic or mechanical means, including information storage and retrieval systems, without permission in writing from the publisher, except by a reviewer who may quote brief passages in a review.

First Edition

All photographs used with the permission of Barbara von Hoffmann, with the exception of the photograph on p. 44, used with the permission of Mordecai Siegal.

The authors are grateful for permission to include the following previously copyrighted material:

Excerpts from *Official Standard for the German Shepherd*, adopted by the German Shepherd Club of America. Copyright © 1991 by the American Kennel Club, Inc. Reprinted by permission of the American Kennel Club, Inc.

Excerpts from *A Guide To Dog Schools* by Ed and Toni Eames. Copyright © 1994 by Ed and Toni Eames. Reprinted by permission of the authors.

Library of Congress Cataloging-in-Publication Data

Siegal, Mordecai.
   The good shepherd : a pet owner's guide to the German shepherd dog / by Mordecai Siegal and Matthew Margolis. — 1st ed.
      p.   cm.
   "The Siegal-Margolis dog library."
   Includes index.
   ISBN 0-316-79019-2
   1. German shepherd dogs.   I. Margolis, Matthew.   II. Title.
SF429.G37S56   1996
636.7'37 — dc20   96-26525

10 9 8 7 6 5 4 3 2 1
RRD-IN
Published simultaneously in Canada by Little, Brown & Company (Canada) Limited

Printed in the United States of America

TO MEMORIES OF

EMILY

Contents

Acknowledgments

The authors are deeply indepted to Sherry Davis and Janell Wilson for their major contributions to this book. They have amply provided us with needed research material and an infrastructure of information that has added greatly to the usefulness of this text. They have imparted their personal knowledge and experience to this work and have greatly enriched it by doing so.

Sherry Davis is a breeder, exhibitor, and expert dog trainer. Her life revolves around her own dogs and the many dogs that are entrusted to her in her professional life. She is the Executive Director of Training for the National Institute of Dog Training in Los Angeles and is responsible for supervising all matters pertaining to that organization's many dog trainers. Her love of all dogs and her understanding of most breeds are reflected through the information she generously provided for this book.

Janell Wilson provided all of the research for the canine health chapters, especially the medical conditions and disorders that dog owners need to know about. We are particularly grateful for her enthusiasm and hard work, which made it possible to present the essential veterinary information that applies specifically to German Shepherd Dogs. She gave us much more information than a book of this scope permits, and we are indebted to her for that. Many thanks are extended for her important contribution. Janell Wilson is the Director of Canine Health at the National Institute of Dog Training.

Much appreciation is given to Jeffrey E. Barlough, D.V.M., Ph.D., of the School of Veterinary Medicine, University of California, Davis, for his kind assistance with various medical aspects of this book.

It is with pleasure, admiration, and gratitude that we acknowledge wildlife and animal photographer Barbara von Hoffmann, of Colorado Springs, for the beautiful photographs she made for this book. Ms. von Hoffmann's sumptuous photographs have been extensively published, appearing in the *AKC Gazette*, on the cover of *Financial World*, and in many other national magazines. They have also graced many beautiful animal calendars and have been included in numerous books published by the Sierra Club and Reader's Digest, to name but a couple.

Ms. von Hoffmann would like us to express her appreciation to Susan Barwig of Canine Training Systems in Littleton, Colorado, for sharing her shutzhund expertise and for helping her shoot the best possible photographs of her champion dogs in posed and working situations. She also expresses her high regard for Ms. Barwig's associate, Doug Calhoun, who worked with the dogs used in her photographs and showed her how they should be trained. She also extends her gratitude to Tom Hendrickson, whose superb dog, Montana Mike, was used extensively in portraits and in schutzhund work. He introduced her to the Schutzhund Club and to the Colorado Springs Canine Corps.

We are especially pleased to add a warm thank you to Ed and Toni Eames for suggesting to us the idea of Guide Dog schools as a source of German Shepherd pets. It was also their fine suggestion that we reprint a small portion of their publication *A Guide to Guide Dog Schools*. Ed and Toni Eames are an inspiration to all who are fortunate enough to meet them, read their column in *Dog World* magazine, or attend their seminars and lectures.

There is no better source of practical information about German Shepherd Dogs than those who breed, handle, and live with them every day of their lives. We prepared an extensive questionnaire that we sent out to a number of top German Shepherd breeders. Those acknowledged here generously answered our questions beyond our expectations. Those named who responded did so in order to give a novice German Shepherd owner the benefit of their experience and wisdom. Many of their answers to our questions confirmed what we had already perceived to be true. However, there were many new insights offered, which were gratefully accepted. Here then are the names of those German Shepherd Dog breeders who are quoted in this book: Ray and Sandra Kozub, KCK Kennels, Sparta, Tennessee; Linda Shepherd La Grave, La Bell Oaks, DeLand, Florida; Doris A. Farrell and Janice LaFountain, Farmil-Katelyn German Shepherds, Roxbury, Connecticut; Cathy Mekula, Epic Shepherds, Winter Park, Florida; Doris and Herb Estabrook, Irrenhaus Kennels, Gardnerville, Nevada; Lynn Fowlston, Reinmiler Kennels, Springville, Tennessee; Kristine Dewey, Ostfriesen German Shepherds, Blue Mounds, Wisconsin; Pat Sears, Whispering Pines Kennels, Temperance, Michigan; Daphne Szczuka, Andaka Kennels, Florissant, Missouri; and Linda A. Novotasky, J-Lyn Shepherds, Middleburg, Florida.

Introduction

The Good Shepherd is more like a person than a dog, but more like a person we always hoped to be. He is smart, hardworking, and completely loyal. For these reasons people rarely refer to their German Shepherds as "my dog" or "our pet." He is more often spoken of as "my friend," "my pal," or "my buddy" — and for good reason. German Shepherds are like no other dogs, because of their distinctive personalities and many outstanding qualities, which have endeared them to all who have ever lived with one. Their presence in any family is dynamic and stirs the deepest emotions. The German Shepherd experience is the dog event of a lifetime.

The breed is well named. When we use the word *shepherd*, we could be referring to a responsible person, alone on the side of a hill, tending a flock of sheep, keeping them together and protecting them from harm. We could also be speaking about a respected leader of a group. As a figure of speech "to shepherd" means "to tend, to guide, to care for, to protect." The German Shepherd Dog does all these things and more. He is also an intelligent worker, a devoted friend, and a happy, warmhearted companion. The Good Shepherd is that rare creature who makes the ideal agree with reality.

As working dogs in the human environment, these even-tempered animals function as police service dogs, military sentries, search-and-rescue dogs, guide dogs for the blind, and companions and protectors for everyone, including children. Wherever they live, whatever they are asked to do, German Shepherd Dogs have been embraced by every nation on earth as the all-around dog for just about every purpose. Few Shepherd people can even conceive of living with another breed. In the United States he is called the *German Shepherd Dog*. In Germany, he is the *Deutsche Schaferhund*. In Great Britain, the *Alsatian*. In this book he is the Good Shepherd.

The Good Shepherd

CHAPTER ONE

Meet the German Shepherd Dog

The Breed in Profile

If you are considering living with a German Shepherd Dog, this profile of the breed will help you make an intelligent decision based on what's right for you and what's right for the dog. If you already live with one, it will be even more useful, by helping you understand this new and interesting member of your family.

The first thing anyone wants to know when deciding which breed to get is what the dog is going to be like. Will he love you and protect your family? Will he fit in with your lifestyle? Will the dog be safe with your family? Will he be fun to live with? Or will he just pee all over the floor, chase cats, and bark at the mailman? If you are in the process of selecting a German Shepherd Dog, it is important to consider the typical behavior of the breed. What will your dog be like? It's an important question.

All dogs, no matter what breed, have many similar behavioral responses. Nature has programmed dogs to behave in specific ways that enable them to survive and reproduce. They are normal instincts and are considered part of basic canine behavior by many researchers and experienced dog experts. However, some typical dog behaviors may be exaggerated, diminished, or completely missing in a specific breed. It is precisely these variations that make many dog breeds different from one another, besides their physical distinctions. The temperament and personality behaviors that are characteristic

of each breed give us a fair idea of what we can expect a particular dog to be like.

Experienced dog people, however, understand that all dogs are born with or develop some personality differences that are unpredictable. Unfortunately, some dogs inherit unexpected temperaments and behavioral responses that are *not* typical of their breed, most often because of poor breeding practices. Nevertheless, you can learn much about the potential behavior of your dog by exploring the breed's typical characteristics. A good place to start is with your breed's original purpose. Learning how and why your breed came into being will give you many insights into your dog's behavior.

The Good Shepherd—Bred to Help

By knowing the original functions of your breed, you can anticipate what your dog's natural inclinations should be because they are, in most cases, passed from one generation to the next. Most dog breeds were developed by humans to perform specialized work for particular needs. Breeders carefully selected for mating those dogs that had a desired size, body type, coat type, or coat color or were gifted with exceptional abilities, behaviors, or temperaments. The purpose was to develop dogs that were best suited for a special job and the living conditions connected with it. There are approximately 400 dog breeds throughout the world, and most are the result of human selection in the breeding process. Hundreds of dog breeds have been carefully and methodically developed for hunting, herding, guarding, protecting, and many other important duties and services, not the least of which is companionship.

The German Shepherd Dog was developed from a variety of randomly bred dogs that were used by German farmers and shepherds to help herd and protect sheep and cattle. Canine herding skills derive from the techniques and strategies that wolves and wild dogs use to hunt for food. A canine hunter finds its prey by sight, smell, and experience. If the hunt involves migrating herd animals, as it often does, the strategy is to stir up the herd by rushing at it from several directions to separate one or more individuals from the rest. Once an animal is isolated and without the protection of the herd, it becomes vulnerable and is almost always brought down for food by the pack.

Although this behavior has been greatly modified and altered in herding dogs through selective breeding and skillful training, the dogs' methodology is based on these instinctive hunting skills and is strikingly similar to that of wolves. Shepherds and drovers cleverly use these instincts to teach herding dogs how to maintain control of their flocks and herds. Of course, the objective of a herding dog is

the exact opposite of a dog that is hunting. Paradoxically, two important objectives of a herding dog are to *prevent* strays from leaving the herd and to *protect* them from predators.

The protective nature of herding and working dogs is basic canine behavior that is greater in some breeds than in others. It is rooted in the instinct to maintain social rank, defend the pack and its territory, and protect the food supply. From this instinct comes the drive to protect the home and family, an instinct stronger in the German Shepherd Dog than in many other breeds. Because of the work they were bred to do, Shepherds are highly territorial dogs and have the size, strength, stamina, and boldness to successfully discourage those who would overstep established boundaries.

Although his name "Shepherd" does imply that his roots were in guarding and herding livestock, his history of service as war hero and status today as police dog and personal protector show him to be the ultimate working dog.

German Shepherd Temperament

The ideal German Shepherd temperament is outgoing, high-energy, playful, friendly, curious, and loving. As adults they become vigilant, self-confident members of the family, as well as instinctive caretakers. They are willing playmates for children and are highly tolerant of energetic games. The Shepherds' desire to participate in the everyday life of the family endears them to all with whom they live.

As adults they are alert, calm, and self-confident. Extreme nervousness is atypical and undesirable. German Shepherds are noted for their intelligence and ability to learn quickly, which makes early training easier and highly desirable.

Although the breed's reputation as a fearless protector and obedient worker is well founded, there are other qualities that are equally outstanding. For example, German Shepherds are gentle, loving, and playful with family and friends. Shepherds that have been properly socialized are friendly to everyone, even strangers if they are themselves friendly and not in violation of

The ideal German Shepherd temperament is outgoing, high-energy, playful, friendly, curious, and loving.

the dog's protective nature. Dogs of this breed are capable of fiercely protecting their family from harm without losing their gentle nature. It is a subtle but important aspect of their temperament.

Of all the dog breeds, Shepherds are probably the most forgiving of human failure. Despite the mistakes their owners make in training or treatment, German Shepherds continue to love their owners unquestioningly and defend them against all harm. Because of their noble manner and their intense loyalty, with few exceptions, their owners always elevate their dogs to the status of "life partner."

Living with Your German Shepherd

The first year with a German Shepherd puppy is an enjoyable time filled with love, laughter, some work, some frustration, a few failures, many successes, and a storehouse of important memories. Keeping up with a typical Shepherd puppy is a challenge because he will be playful and eager to get into everything. His intelligence and friskiness are a formula for mischief if the young dog is not supervised at all times. Shepherd puppies are energy in motion. However, high energy is the engine that propels a working dog's drive to perform well and do his best. Despite their energy, some Shepherds are picky eaters. Others eat anything put in front of them. There is no way to anticipate these tendencies.

German Shepherd puppies are young, gawky dogs that trot awkwardly as they run to you. Their thick paws move up and down in rapid motion as the puppies canter quickly like new colts. With one ear up and another folded down or to the side, these funny, immature bumblers are difficult to picture as the large, agile, powerhouse dogs they become. They are irresistible as puppies and adolescents because they love to play, to please, and to shower you with attention. A well-bred, properly raised German Shepherd should like everybody, should be social with people and animals alike, and adapt well to all members of the family.

A puppy will follow you all day long, especially if you are the person whom he bonded with. Bonding with your dog is the key to liv-

Shepherds that have been properly socialized are friendly to everyone.

ing happily with him. (Please read Chapter Four, "The Shepherd Bond.") Whoever becomes the caretaker for the first two weeks is probably going to be the dog's number-one person in the family and will develop the strongest bond. If there is another dog in the family, it is important *not* to keep them together all of the time in the first few weeks. By spending balanced time with *everyone,* the new dog will bond with each individual member of the family rather than with the other dog, to the exclusion of everyone else.

The most desirable German Shepherds start out as high-energy puppies, which is so necessary for working dogs. They love to play, especially with a tossed ball or a tug toy, and enjoy a vigorous run. This playful, happy behavior should be indulged and even encouraged. Shepherd puppies are also very curious. They love to get into everything, stop suddenly and sniff around, and check out anything that is new or appears to be strange or out of the ordinary. This curiosity foreshadows their natural tracking ability and protective behavior as adult dogs.

Typical Shepherd puppies are very alert and investigate with cheerful enthusiasm every new person who enters their domain. They want to know who you are, what you are, and what you are doing. Shepherds are adorable when they are young and small. They appear to be less than graceful and lovably clownish as they enter their adolescent period, which is between five and twelve months of age. German Shepherds are irresistible at this stage and easy to hold and hug, allowing them anything they ask for, including your bed (which means, of course, they will *always* be on your bed). Although their eyes are keenly alert, Shepherd puppies have a soft, soulful quality to them, especially when they want something.

With few exceptions, Shepherds respond brilliantly to every form of dog training imaginable, which is why they can be Guide Dogs, Therapy Dogs, Search and Rescue Dogs, protection dogs, and do all the things that dogs can be trained to do.

When living with a German Shepherd, it is a good idea to consider your goals while the dog is still young and easy to manage. Simply wanting a companion animal for the fun and friendship involved is not too demanding. But if you are interested in any of the dog sports, such as obedience trials, or in putting your Shepherd to work as a protection dog, it is best to make that decision as soon as possible, while the dog is very young. Training for obedience trials or protection work requires a lot of time and hard work. If you begin *after* the dog has fully matured, it is much more difficult to manage him at ninety pounds with a mind of his own. Training should begin soon after you get the dog.

If you are going to live with a German Shepherd, it is essential that he grow into a friendly, social animal. To accomplish this, you must get him out into the world as often as you can in the first year and throughout his life. Take him with you shopping and on errands at every opportunity available. To be a friendly, social dog, he must be exposed to a wide variety of people, places, noises, and different human and animal situations. If you keep him home exclusively and limit his relationships to your family, you will be in danger of creating an aggressive, dangerous dog. Some German Shepherd Dogs have aggressive behavior problems because their owners have kept them away from everybody and only allowed them to love their family. Their intention was to create a dog that protects them, which is the wrong way to accomplish this goal. It is a fact that the best guard dogs are friendly dogs that have been socialized and professionally trained. Properly trained protection dogs can go anywhere and be trusted with anybody. Aggressive dogs that cannot be controlled must be kept away when a friend or relative enters your home. If your dog is social, he can enter any situation and act appropriately in the presence of a good guy or a bad guy.

It's never too early to begin thinking about obedience and protection training.

It does not take too long to discover that German Shepherds shed a great deal and must be brushed frequently to get rid of their loose hair. However, it is impossible to avoid *all* their shedding hair, which inevitably gets all over your house, your clothes, and your car. Please read Grooming and Hygiene in Chapter Ten, "Keeping Your German Shepherd Dog Healthy" (page 167). In addition, they are sloppy eaters who like to move around their food bowls while gulping down their meals and should be fed in a place where spilled food will not upset you. The truth is that German Shepherds are not the ideal breed for those who are fastidious and for whom a spotless home is more important than their dog. Bear in mind that dogs, like people, are not perfect and have many positive qualities that more than compensate for a few of their negative ones.

German Shepherds get along well with children so long as they are raised with the children and are familiar with their energetic behavior. In the beginning the Shepherd puppy thinks of itself as just another one of the kids in the family. Puppies and children will all play together, sleep together, and even have arguments with one another over food, toys, and other personal possessions. The bonding between Shepherds and children (and your children's friends) is charming and reassuring. Of course, a German Shepherd Dog matures much sooner than a child and becomes more responsible and protective. At a certain point a recently matured Shepherd will pay more attention to the one person in the family who feeds, walks, and trains the dog. Early bonding with that person dictates this behavior. However, the dog never stops loving and relating to the youngsters in the family. If the dog has always slept in a child's room, for example, he will continue to do so. Shepherds and children are great together.

If you acquire a Shepherd before you start your family, it is essential that you socialize him early in life by getting him out into the world as much as possible to meet children and other people. A dog that never leaves his backyard, is not usually walked down the street, or is not taken anywhere in a car except to go to the vet is more likely to growl and threaten anyone he does not know, including children. You may feel protected by creating a dog that does not trust anyone he doesn't know, but you will never enjoy any other aspects of living with a dog. The problem is that not all strangers are bad people—for example, letter carriers, utility workers, friends, neighbors, and children. A social, friendly dog is the best watchdog. He will always be by your side, no matter who comes into your home.

Living with your German Shepherd means you should be living with the sweetest, most lovable dog in the world, who will, by the way, protect you *when it is appropriate* without being transformed into a dangerous animal by lack of human contact.

What the Breeders Say

It is interesting to learn what experienced German Shepherd Dog breeders think and whether they agree with one another. In a questionnaire sent to a number of active breeders, the first thing asked was to describe the typical personality traits of the breed. These are their responses:

"Very loyal, loving, and protective to his or her family. Generally quiet, calm dogs to live with and easy to train because of their desire to please the ones they love. They need some exercise and firm training. They can assume dominant personality traits if the owner does not establish a 'leader' role. Harsh discipline is very seldom necessary."

"Loyalty, attentiveness, courage, fighting spirit, protective. The Shepherd should be a true working dog."

"[American-bred German Shepherd only] I don't know about German dogs. Loving and affectionate, but protective when necessary without formal training. Super-intelligent and quick to learn."

"Energy, lots of energy, enthusiasm, always ready to go ahead on into life. Shepherds are funny, so very smart, very bonded, and in tune with their person. They are proud, with that 'look at me' attitude."

"Alert, fun-loving, eager to learn, a great desire to be your companion and best friend. Most of all, intelligent."

"The typical personality traits of the Shepherd are steady nerves, being attentive, loyalty to his family, calm and self-assured, as well as courage to protect. He should give the impression of strength and intelligence and an abundance of vitality. He should be willing to carry out his work, no matter

Living with your German Shepherd means you should be living with the sweetest, most lovable dog in the world.

what it consists of, with enthusiasm. He should be observant, obedient, and a great all-round dog to live with. He should be especially at ease around children, other animals, and adults, yet be wary of strangers, ready to protect if the need arises."

"The typical personality traits of the breed include a happy, outgoing nature with a ready willingness to please. They are highly intelligent and are easily motivated to learn new tasks. German Shepherds seem to have an intrinsic desire to keep themselves busy in ways that seem to reflect on the heritage they were bred for. For example, guarding behavior will be shown with another puppy or dog by playing ferociously, yet never actually getting mean with the other dog. And if it is a puppy trying to get the stick or bone, somehow they manage to get it away without any harm coming to them.

"In my large fenced yard it is a great game with the dogs to protect their territory with barking, no matter what the perceived threat. Birds are chased with great determination, and even butterflies are shown no mercy. On hot summer afternoons several will nearly do somersaults jumping straight up in the air after butterflies.

"German Shepherds also exhibit happiness when their owners are busy and they also are somehow involved, even if it is only by providing companionship. They love to walk, ride in cars, and follow you from room to room. They are very adept at reading their owners' behavior, and changing clothes, getting a purse, or car keys will set them off by jumping in the air and running to the door. In fact, I would say this sets them apart from other breeds in the intensity with which they watch you for visual clues. It is also a key factor which makes them so highly trainable."

"Very loyal, extremely intelligent, protective, excellent family pet."

Nontypical Traits

It is important to understand that some dogs are *not* typical of the breed and create a false impression about breed characteristics. Occasionally a Shepherd is born that is not typical, and it can only be considered a genetic misfortune. This has happened to most breeders at one time or another despite their experience and good intentions.

However, *most* dogs that are not typical of their breed are the result of bad breeding practices. Bad examples of the breed are most often the result of ignorance, apathy, the irresponsible pursuit of profit, and greed. When a breed becomes as popular as the German Shepherd Dog, it is always in danger of being exploited in an attempt to satisfy the great demand by overbreeding.

The law of supply and demand motivates profiteers to mate all German Shepherds they can get their hands on, without the selectivity necessary for a good breeding program. In that situation there is no thought of the health or behavior of the dogs that are mated. Dogs that may have inherited diseases, disorders, poor breed type, or bad temperament are most likely going to pass on those negative factors to their puppies. Once atypical breed traits or health problems are established in the gene pool, it is anyone's guess which future puppies will inherit those problems.

Other reasons for atypical breed traits that appear in Shepherds may be harmful circumstances and events that have occurred in the dog's life. Among these could have been harsh and unhealthy living conditions, abusive treatment, no training, improper training, little or no medical attention, isolation from people, or serious mistakes made by uninformed breeders or dog owners.

What the Breeders Say

Breeders of German Shepherds were also asked in the questionnaire, "Which traits would be *atypical* of the breed?" Once again there is much agreement among them. Here are their replies:

> *"Shyness, aggression."*
> *"Aggressive without provocation, nervous, timid."*
> *"Nervousness, shyness, viciousness."*
> *"Unsteady nerves, overaggressiveness, nervousness, shyness, hiding behind their master with tail tucked between their legs. Lack of confidence in any situation."*
> *"Traits that are nontypical include aggression toward the owner or*

children. While there may be many instances of these things happening, I suspect most are the result of prior abuse and poor treatment."

"The German Shepherd Dog must not be timid or nervous, nor should he be overly aggressive. Lack of confidence is not typical of good character. Any deficiencies that indicate shyness must be considered as a serious fault. The ideal dog is a working animal with an incorruptible character combined with body and gait suitable for the work that is its primary purpose. All of these characteristics can be found in the AKC Standard for German Shepherd Dogs."

Searching for a German Shepherd Puppy

Selecting the best German Shepherd for you and your family requires some homework and some legwork. Read as much as possible about the breed (in books, articles, pamphlets) and then go out and meet the Shepherd people (exhibitors, breeders, veterinarians, dog trainers, groomers, pet owners) and talk to them, asking them all the questions you can think of. These activities are not only interesting and informative but also great fun. If you do so, you will become capable of selecting the best puppy available. You will also be quite proud of yourself and your new dog.

Although dogs are everywhere and getting one is easy, getting the *right* one is a little harder. Acquiring a dog on impulse can be a disaster waiting to happen. Some people become pet owners by chance. This may happen when a puppy is purchased as a last-minute Christmas or birthday gift or if you give in to the emotional appeal of a young puppy cunningly placed in your arms. Getting a dog in such a way often leads to anger and sadness. Of course, many people have successfully found pet dogs without much fuss and have been very happy with the outcome. Nevertheless, the risk of failure is high, and it can lead to heartbreak for everyone concerned. When selecting a German Shepherd puppy, the dangers are purchasing a dog with a genetically inherited medical problem, such as hip dysplasia, or a severe behavioral defect, such as shyness or excessive aggression. The best chance of avoiding this is to learn how to select a sound, healthy dog from a reputable breeding source.

Before selecting a puppy, attend All-Breed or Specialty dog shows featuring the German Shepherd Dog. Show listings can be obtained directly from the American Kennel Club, the United Kennel Club, or the German Shepherd Club of America. Attending a show will give you an opportunity to see good examples of the breed and talk to owners, handlers, and breeders. At a dog show you will definitely find many sources for high-quality German Shepherds. You can also find breeder ads in the popular dog magazines, such as *Dogs USA, Dog Fancy,* the AKC *Gazette, Dog World,* or *Blood Lines* (UKC). Write or call the American Kennel Club for its breeder-referral information or for the address of the current secretary of the German Shepherd Club of America, from whom you can obtain a list of German Shepherd breeders in your region. Write to the American Kennel Club, 51 Madison Avenue, New York, New York 10010; or to the United Kennel Club, 100 East Kilgore Road, Kalamazoo, Michigan 49001-5596.

Selecting a Good Puppy

Puppies are appealing and huggable. On first sight you will want to take them all home because it is difficult to choose one over another. Their large, brown eyes seem to say, "Take me. I love you." Shepherd puppies are tantalizing and make it almost impossible to make an intelligent selection. Apart from noting personality differences and which one looks best, the most important criteria for selecting a pet dog are health and temperament. It is in your best interest to know the difference between a puppy that is healthy and of good temperament from one that is not.

Most breeders proudly show likely buyers a pedigree, which is an impressive-looking document outlining a puppy's parentage, or family tree, going back at least three generations. It will tell you a lot about a puppy if you are familiar with German Shepherds of high

Shepherd puppies are tantalizing and make it almost impossible to make an intelligent selection.

quality by name and with the kennels that produced them. It is a meaningless document to those who know little or nothing about such matters as "foundation stock," past and present German Shepherd champions, and the kennels that produced the dogs mentioned in the pedigree.

However, most breeders are eager to explain a puppy's pedigree to you if you show the slightest interest. There is something to be gained by reading the document even if you don't understand all of it. For example, if there is at least one dog listed in the pedigree with a Champion title, it is an indication that the puppy comes from a line of quality breeding. Of course, you may still get a great dog without a champion in the family tree, especially if it is to be a companion animal. If you have done your homework, you will be able to recognize a few of the names of the kennels with important reputations. One could very easily show up on a pedigree.

Another important document a breeder or retailer may show you is an AKC registration certificate for the litter of puppies you are looking at or for an individual puppy. *An official American Kennel Club or United Kennel Club registration certificate is a document that is supposed to prove a dog's purebred status. That is all it means. It does not guarantee in any way the quality of a dog or puppy. It is important to understand this.*

It is far more useful to see the mother or father of the puppies you are looking at. One or the other should be available if you are visiting a kennel. This is where your experience at dog shows and the books and pictures you have examined serves you. If the puppies' parents appear to be in good health and seem to have an even temperament, it is likely that their puppies will grow up to be somewhat like them. If you have read the *Official Standard for the German Shepherd Dog* from the American Kennel Club (reprinted at the end of this chapter), you should be able to tell if the dogs come close to it or not.

Because most puppies are bought as companion animals, a breeder may refer you to a "pet quality" dog rather than one with "show potential." Do not be put off by this. Many breeders will not sell a puppy with show potential to someone who wants a pet. Those puppies are usually reserved for the breeder if he or she shows dogs or for someone who will "campaign" them at dog shows and try to win the fifteen points necessary for a Champion title. This is an expensive and time-consuming activity. Dogs that earn the title Champion help establish a kennel's reputation and the quality of its breeding program. For the breeder it is a matter of pride and economics. However, there are a few breeders who are more interested in selling their puppies than in telling you the truth about such matters as a puppy's show potential. Such a breeder may say, "All my dogs have show potential," which is technically correct. But if you are looking for a "show dog," you must get expert advice.

"Pet quality" puppies are wonderful dogs. Important matters of health and temperament are different considerations from a puppy's "show potential." Such dogs have simply not met every aspect of the Official Standard and have limited chances for winning dog shows, which should not matter to anyone who just wants a dog to live with. Pet-quality dogs are the best companion animals in the world.

Choosing a Healthy Puppy

The most important consideration when selecting a puppy is its good health. A simple set of observations when looking at a litter of puppies or at an individual dog will help enormously. It is essential to be as objective as possible and try to discover any medical problems *before* you make your selection. Nothing short of a veterinary examination can accurately reveal all aspects of a puppy's health. You are entirely on your own when making your puppy selection.

Still, you do not have to be a health-care professional to know when you are looking at puppies in good health. A healthy litter of puppies should be frisky and outgoing; they should appear to be enjoying themselves and glow with good health. If there is one puppy in the group that is sluggish, upset-looking, walks or runs with a limp, has an exceptionally unhealthy-looking coat, or shows any obvious signs of bad health, be cautious about your selection.

The coat. The puppy coat should be soft, bright, and healthy-looking, without clumps, mats, or bald patches. A coat in bad condition can be a sign of disease, parasites (worms, fleas, ticks), physical stress, emotional stress, or an unhealthy environment. A healthy puppy's coat should be loose, supple, and have no bald patches of hair or dandruff-like flakes.

The skin. The skin underneath should not have any damaged surfaces, scaly areas, or sores. A puppy's skin or haircoat should not show evidence of fleas, which resembles grains of salt and pepper. Active fleas may or may not be visible. Your new puppy should have clean, smooth, undamaged skin.

The eyes. Healthy eyes should be clear, clean, and alert, with no excessive watering or sensitivity to light. Unnatural markings or inconsistent coloring on the corneas (the outer covering of the eye) may indicate corneal ulcers, which appear as colorless, indented spots. They are considered to be a serious medical condition. If a puppy's eyes seem to tear excessively or if he continually rubs his eyes with a paw, he probably has a medical problem.

The ears. The ears of a German Shepherd puppy should be clean, particularly on the inner surface. Dirty-looking or waxy material inside may mean the puppy has ear mites. Ear mites are minute white specks that move. They are common parasites in dogs and cause infection. If a puppy shakes its head excessively, scratches and rubs its ears, and behaves in a restless manner, it is very likely infected with mites. Veterinary care is necessary.

To test for deafness, slap your hands behind a puppy's ears. Rattle some keys loudly where he cannot see them. If there is no response, it is likely the puppy does not have normal hearing.

Choosing a Puppy with a Good Temperament

Good temperament in the German Shepherd Dog is essential, and puppies should be selected with this as a primary consideration. Shy or overly aggressive dogs should be passed over as well as puppies who have a parent that shows questionable temperament.

The German Shepherd puppy you choose should be lively, with a friendly, outgoing attitude. Avoid a puppy that is shy or fearful if he is already seven to eight weeks old. Even at this young age, the typical German Shepherd temperament of self-assurance is apparent. An aloof presence with strangers is not correct in a German Shepherd puppy. Such a puppy may prove to be unsocial as an adult and develop into an overprotective adult that is unselective in his aggres-

Even at this young age, the typical German Shepherd temperament of self-assurance is apparent.

sion. Choose a puppy that is active and attentive to your voice and presence. This is your best possibility for a dog that will grow up and become your best friend and protector.

When selecting a puppy, temperament is one of the most important aspects to consider. This has an important bearing on emotional stability and the potential for acceptable behavior as an adult dog. A German Shepherd puppy that is going to be a companion animal should be playful, enthusiastic, curious, eager, self-confident, energetic, and affectionate. Do not look for the most aggressive puppy unless you are looking for a show prospect; in that case, choose the boldest puppy of the litter. A bold puppy is not an aggressive puppy, it is a dog that wants attention and is not timid about getting it. Such a canine personality is ideal for winning in the show ring.

Shepherd puppies should come right up to you and lick your face. Normal puppies love everybody. If one puppy in a litter is described as "calm," it is a substitution for the word *shy*. Normal Shepherds do not become truly calm until they are three years old. This is true of most breeds. All puppies should be active and all over the place; if not, something is wrong.

Beware of shy, timid, or overly aggressive puppies. What is heartwarming or cute at twelve weeks can make you quite unhappy at six or eight months of age. A shy puppy may cringe, cower, or snarl and growl when petted, picked up, or cornered in any way. Shepherd puppies that are not curious, energetic, playful, or eager to greet you are either sick or atypical of the breed and should be avoided. (Of course, puppies can also be tired at the time of viewing and may simply want to take a nap.) When considering buying a puppy, try to imagine what he will be like as a grown dog. Look for an outgoing, friendly dog who comes right up to you and does not hide in the corner or run with fear.

Do not choose a puppy with a *shy* temperament. Shy dogs grow up to be abnormally frightened of anyone or anything that is unfamiliar. They do their best to avoid most people, animals, or changes in their environment.

Another temperament type to avoid is the *aggressive* dog. Puppies that growl seriously from their throat are warning you that they will bite. That is unacceptable and undesirable behavior and indicative of an aggressive puppy who will grow into an aggressive, possibly dangerous dog. If you are suspicious of overly aggressive behavior, place the puppy on his back and hold him there for ten or fifteen seconds. A puppy with a potential behavior problem will growl, snarl, howl, bark, and even snap and bite to get back on his feet. Do not choose this puppy as a pet.

Puppies that have been handled by humans on a regular basis after three weeks of age have been "socialized." This means they are more adaptable to living with humans and accept obedience training easily. If they have been allowed to remain with their mother and litter mates for seven weeks, they are likely to adjust easily to other dogs as well as humans (provided they have been socialized).

The transference of genetic characteristics plays an important role in dog behavior, too. If the puppies' mother and father are at ease with strangers, congenial, outgoing, and friendly, it is likely that their puppies will be the same way, provided they have been handled properly.

When observing a litter of puppies, kneel at floor level and observe which ones are curious about you, friendly toward you, want you to touch them. With the breeder's permission, lift them in your arms, one at a time, to see if they are at ease with you. Hold each puppy in your arms with the belly facing up. If the dog submits with ease and pleasure, his temperament is just fine. If he squirms desperately to get away, he may be aggressive or nervous. If he whines and whimpers, he may be shy. A normal puppy will either thrash about playfully or settle in and enjoy the contact. He should follow you around when you set him down on the floor. Try playing with him. A friendly, outgoing puppy should enjoy playing with you. He may roll on his back and flail his paws in the air or place your finger in his mouth or try to climb on you and lick your face.

Try tossing something for the puppies to retrieve. They should respond well to this. Get them to come to you by clapping your hands. Observe how social they are with one another. Pay attention to whether they interact reasonably with their brothers and sisters. Avoid a loner or a puppy that is a bully around the food or in play.

A new puppy should be taken to his new home at seven or eight weeks of age. This makes bonding with the young dog easier and more successful. Waiting longer than eight weeks makes the process more difficult unless the puppy has interacted with many different people. There is more to canine health than clear eyes and a glossy coat. A happy, self-assured puppy that delights in the company of humans is likely to enjoy good health and long life.

The Official *German* Shepherd

Serious breeders and exhibitors (those who compete at dog shows) work hard to produce dogs that compare favorably with the American Kennel Club or United Kennel Club's Official Standard for their breed. This is not only appropriate but essential, because these are members of the *Dog Fancy* who have the responsibility of preserving (and improving) the qualities of their breed, which include physical characteristics and behavioral traits.

Originally, German Shepherd Dogs were registered by the American Kennel Club in the Working Group. In 1983 the AKC split the Working Group because of its immense size, adding a seventh classification, the Herding Group. The German Shepherd was reclassified and placed in the new Herding Group. The decision was controversial and continues to provoke disagreement among breeders.

Although pet owners rarely have the same concerns about their dogs as breeders and exhibitors, some considerations apply equally when selecting a good dog. Many potential pet owners are not sure what the breed of choice should actually look like or what kind of behavior to expect. Attending canine competitions (the *Dog Sport*) involving obedience trials, field trials, hunting tests, agility, and other contests may be helpful but the most popular event is the dog show. The dog show, as sanctioned by the American Kennel Club, is referred to as a *conformation show.*

It is a competition concerned with a dog's skeletal form, musculature, movement and gait, coat color and pattern, and overall appearance, health, and behavior.

In a dog show the dogs' various physical structures are judged against guidelines detailed in the Official Standard. It is not a beauty contest, although many dogs entered in dog shows are among the most beautiful-looking in the world. The "conformation" of a dog pertains to overall appearance

and physical formation, involving both its individual characteristics and the sum total of those characteristics as a well-balanced
composite.

American Kennel Club judges examine each dog in competition
and decide how closely it compares with the descriptions in the Official Standard for the breed. The dogs that are judged to be closest to
the written standard win points for a championship title (fifteen required) in addition to awards and prizes. Although the Official Standard for any breed represents an ideal, it is used by breeders,
exhibitors, and show judges as an important guideline for evaluating
dogs within a breed.

It is worth the effort for potential pet owners to read the Official
Standard of the breed of dog they want. How else can you determine
if the puppy being considered comes close to the type of dog you
have your heart set on? Before you read the standard, however, there
are a few pointers that can be of help with the puppy selection.

Size. The German Shepherd is a large, well-muscled active dog
noted for its beautiful movement; famous extended, or flying, trot;
and the ability to function as an agile, working animal in all climates.
With this in mind, you should not assume that the bigger the German
Shepherd, the better. Oversized or giant dogs may lack endurance
and appear sloppy and sluggish in performance. Even though all
puppies appear to have big feet, long ears, and long tails, they will
even out with maturity. An eighty-pound adult in working weight is
not too small. Females are generally several pounds lighter and
somewhat shorter than males.

Coat color. The true German Shepherd is a powerfully built animal
with a wash-and-wear coat. The coat color of a German Shepherd
should be rich and neither unbroken nor splotchy and may be black,
black and tan, black and red, black and gray or silver, sable, or gray
with brown markings. White is unacceptable in the show ring in all
countries. All colors may compete in AKC performance events, such
as obedience, tracking, and agility. The coat color will not affect the
German Shepherd's role as a companion animal.

A long coat is caused by a recessive gene carried in many normal-coated German Shepherds. While faulted in the ring for lack of texture and undercoat, it in no way affects the dog's beauty or intelligence.

Eyes. Look for eyes that are dark, darker than the coat color. Eyes that are too light or have a startled look are untypical of the breed and should be avoided. Medium almond-shaped eyes are preferable to large or round eyes.

Ears. German Shepherd puppies are born with their ears down. When you select your puppy, the ears may still be down or starting to come up, depending on the puppy's age. Look for medium-sized ears with strong muscles that will fit the structure of the head. The erect ears of the German Shepherd Dog are distinctive and help create its noble look. Do not mishandle a puppy's ears. Refrain from bending or stroking the sensitive cartilage of the young dog's ears. A Shepherd's ears may grow erratically and stay up, go down, and then go up again throughout the first year.

Official breed standards are created by the various national breed clubs and reviewed and approved by the American Kennel Club. With that in mind and with the generous permission of the American Kennel Club, we reprint here the Official Standard for the German Shepherd Dog.

Official Standard for the GERMAN SHEPHERD DOG

(adopted by the German Shepherd Dog Club of America and approved by The American Kennel Club, Inc.)

General Appearance—The first impression of a good German Shepherd Dog is that of a strong, agile, well muscled animal, alert and full of life. It is well balanced, with harmonious development of the forequarter and hindquarter. The dog is longer than tall, deep-bodied, and presents an outline of smooth curves rather than angles. It looks substantial and not spindly, giving the impression, both at rest and in motion, of muscular fitness and nimbleness without any look of clumsiness or soft living. The ideal dog is stamped with a look of quality and nobility—difficult to define, but unmistakable when present. Secondary sex characteristics are strongly marked, and every animal gives a definite impression of masculinity or femininity, according to its sex.

Temperament—The breed has a distinctive personality marked by direct and fearless, but not hostile, expression, self-confidence and a certain aloofness that does not lend itself to immediate and indiscriminate friendships. The dog must be approachable, quietly standing its ground and showing confidence and willingness to meet overtures without itself making them. It is poised, but when the occasion demands, eager and alert; both fit and willing to serve in its capacity as companion, watchdog, blind leader, herding dog, or guardian, whichever the circumstances may demand. The dog must not be timid, shrinking behind its master or handler; it should not be nervous, looking about or upward with anxious expression or showing nervous reactions, such as tucking of tail, to strange sounds or sights. Lack of confidence under any surroundings is not typical of good character. Any of the above deficiencies in character which indicate shyness must be penalized as very *serious faults* and any dog exhibiting pronounced indications of these must be excused from the ring. It must be possible for the judge to observe the teeth and to determine that both testicles are descended. Any dog that attempts to bite the judge must be *disqualified*. The ideal dog is a working animal with an incorruptible character combined with body and gait suitable for the arduous work that constitutes its primary purpose.

Size, Proportion, Substance—The desired *height* for males at the top of the highest point of the shoulder blade is 24 to 26 inches; and for bitches, 22 to 24 inches.

The German Shepherd Dog is longer than tall, with the most desirable *proportion* as 10 to 8½. The length is measured from the point of the prosternum or breastbone to the rear edge of the pelvis, the ischial tuberosity. The desirable long proportion is not derived from a long back, but from overall length with relation to height, which is achieved by length of forequarter and length of withers and hindquarter, viewed from the side.

Head — The *head* is noble, cleanly chiseled, strong without coarseness, but above all not fine, and in proportion to the body. The head of the male is distinctly masculine, and that of the bitch distinctly feminine.

The *expression* keen, intelligent and composed. *Eyes* of medium size, almond shaped, set a little obliquely and not protruding. The color is as dark as possible. *Ears* are moderately pointed, in proportion to the skull, open toward the front, and carried erect when at attention, the ideal carriage being one in which the center lines of the ears, viewed from the front, are parallel to each other and perpendicular to the ground. A dog with cropped or hanging ears must be *disqualified*.

Seen from the front the forehead is only moderately arched, and the *skull* slopes into the long, wedge-shaped muzzle without abrupt stop. The *muzzle* is long and strong, and its topline is parallel to the topline of the skull. *Nose* black. A dog with a nose that is not predominantly black must be *disqualified*. The lips are firmly fitted. Jaws are strongly developed. *Teeth* — 42 in number — 20 upper and 22 lower — are strongly developed and meet in a scissors bite in which part of the inner surface of the upper incisors meet and engage part of the outer surface of the lower incisors. An overshot jaw or a level bite is undesirable. An undershot jaw is a *disqualifying fault*. Complete dentition is to be preferred. Any missing teeth other than first premolars is a *serious fault*.

Neck, Topline, Body — The *neck* is strong and muscular, cleancut and relatively long, proportionate in size to the head and without loose folds of skin. When the dog is at attention or excited, the head is raised and the neck carried high; otherwise typical carriage of the head is forward rather than up and but little higher than the top of the shoulders, particularly in motion.

Topline—The *withers* are higher than and sloping into the level back. The *back* is straight, very strongly developed without sag or roach, and relatively short. The whole structure of the *body* gives an impression of depth and solidity without bulkiness.

Chest—Commencing at the prosternum, it is well filled and carried well down between the legs. It is deep and capacious, never shallow, with ample room for lungs and heart, carried well forward, with the prosternum showing ahead of the shoulder in profile. *Ribs* well sprung and long, neither barrel-shaped nor too flat, and carried down to a sternum which reaches to the elbows. Correct ribbing allows the elbows to move back freely when the dog is at a trot. Too round causes interference and throws the elbows out; too flat or short causes pinched elbows. Ribbing is carried well back so that the loin is relatively short. *Abdomen* firmly held and not paunchy. The bottom line is only moderately tucked up in the loin.

Loin—Viewed from the top, broad and strong. Undue length between the last rib and the thigh, when viewed from the side, is undesirable. *Croup* long and gradually sloping.

Tail bushy, with the last vertebra extended at least to the hock joint. It is set smoothly into the croup and low rather than high. At rest, the tail hangs in a slight curve like a saber. A slight hook—sometimes carried to one side—is faulty only to the extent that it mars general appearance. When the dog is excited or in motion, the curve is accentuated and the tail raised, but it should never be curled forward beyond a vertical line. Tails too short, or with clumpy ends due to ankylosis, are *serious faults*. A dog with a docked tail must be *disqualified*.

Forequarters—The shoulder blades are long and obliquely angled, laid on flat and not placed forward. The upper arm joins the shoulder blade at about a right angle. Both the upper arm and the shoulder blade are well muscled. The forelegs, viewed from all sides, are straight and the bone oval rather than round. The pasterns are strong and springy and angulated at approximately a 25-degree angle from the vertical. Dewclaws on the forelegs may be removed, but are normally left on.

The *feet* are short, compact with toes well arched, pads thick and firm, nails short and dark.

Hindquarters — The whole assembly of the thigh, viewed from the side, is broad, with both upper and lower thigh well muscled, forming as nearly as possible a right angle. The upper thigh bone parallels the shoulder blade while the lower thigh bone parallels the upper arm. The metatarsus (the unit between the hock joint and the foot) is short, strong and tightly articulated. The dewclaws, if any, should be removed from the hind legs. Feet as in front.

Coat — The ideal dog has a double coat of medium length. The outer coat should be as dense as possible, hair straight, harsh and lying close to the body. A slightly wavy outer coat, often of wiry texture, is permissible. The head, including the inner ear and foreface, and the legs and paws are covered with short hair, and the neck with longer and thicker hair. The rear of the forelegs and hind legs has somewhat longer hair extending to the pastern and hock, respectively. *Faults* in coat include soft, silky, too long outer coat, woolly, curly, and open coat.

Color — The German Shepherd Dog varies in color, and most colors are permissible. Strong rich colors are preferred. Pale, washed-out colors and blues or livers are *serious faults*. A white dog must be *disqualified*.

Gait — A German Shepherd Dog is a trotting dog, and its structure has been developed to meet the requirements of its work. *General Impression* — The gait is outreaching, elastic, seemingly without effort, smooth and rhythmic, covering the maximum amount of ground with the minimum number of steps. At a walk it covers a great deal of ground, with long stride of both hind legs and forelegs. At a trot the dog covers still more ground with even longer stride, and moves powerfully but easily, with coordination and balance so that the gait appears to be the steady motion of a well-lubricated machine. The feet travel close to the ground on both forward reach and backward push. In order to achieve ideal movement of this kind, there must be good muscular development and ligamentation. The hindquarters deliver, through the back, a powerful forward thrust which slightly lifts the whole animal and drives the body forward. Reaching far under, and passing the imprint left by the front foot, the hind foot takes hold of the ground; then hock, stifle and upper thigh come into play and sweep back, the stroke of the hind leg finishing with the foot still close to the ground in a smooth follow-through. The overreach of the hindquarter usually necessitates one hind foot passing outside and the other hind foot passing inside the track of the forefeet, and such action is not faulty unless the locomotion is crabwise with the dog's body sideways out of the normal straight line.

Transmission — The typical smooth, flowing gait is maintained with great strength and firmness of back. The whole effort of the hindquarter is transmitted to the forequarter through the loin, back and withers. At full trot, the back must remain firm and level without sway, roll, whip or roach. Unlevel topline with withers lower than the hip is a *fault*. To compensate for the forward motion imparted by the hindquarters, the shoulder should open to its full extent. The forelegs should reach out close to the ground in a long stride in harmony with that of the hindquarters. The dog does not track on widely separated parallel lines, but brings the feet inward toward the middle line of the body when trotting, in order to maintain balance. The feet track closely but do not strike or cross over. Viewed from the front, the front legs function from the shoulder joint to the pad in a straight line. Viewed from the rear, the hind legs function from the hip joint to the pad in a straight line. Faults of gait, whether from front, rear or side, are to be considered very *serious faults*.

Disqualifications

Cropped or hanging ears.
Dogs with noses not predominantly black.
Undershot jaw.
Docked tail.
White dogs.
Any dog that attempts to bite the judge.

Approved February 11, 1978
Reformatted July 11, 1994

CHAPTER TWO

A Bit of History

The written histories and origins of dog breeds come from kennel records, documents, letters, anecdotes, previously written breed histories, or stories passed down from one generation to another. Some modern breeds of obscure origin have been attributed to specific periods in ancient history because of fossils of animals assumed to be dogs or because of similar-looking dogs depicted on stone carvings, artifacts, coins, or works of art from the period.

Other breed histories may stand as part fact, part legend, and part guesswork, or as insupportable speculation. As in all facets of history, facts are elusive and difficult to verify. It is probably best to accept such breed chronicles as historical guideposts. However, they are all interesting to read and enjoyable to consider. Despite some fanciful writing of the past concerning the ancient origins of the German Shepherd, its origin as a breed goes back only to 1899.

The German Shepherd derives and was developed from an assortment of sheep- and farm dogs that successfully worked in various parts of Germany for centuries. They could be grouped informally as "German Sheepdogs." It is important to understand that they were quite varied, with no fixed type. Their coat was long or short, smooth or wiry, with colors ranging from white to gray, from black to black and tan, brindle (black hairs mixed with lighter gray or brown), and even piebald (large patches of two or more colors, usually black and white). Some had erect ears (the classic German Shepherd look); others had tipped (the tops bend forward, Collie-like) or dropped ears (hanging down, as is typical of hounds, retrievers, setters, and spaniels).

No matter what they looked like, these informally bred dogs were highly prized by German farmers and livestock breeders, who had used them for hundreds of years as herding workers. By the end of the nineteenth century, however, the method for moving sheep and cattle changed: it had become cheaper and more efficient to transport them by railroad. Herding dogs were no longer needed to move sheep on long drives to the marketplace. They had become obsolete.

About the same time that herding dogs lost their original purpose, dog shows began to grow rapidly in popularity. This was a significant turn of events that began the process of creating the German Shepherd Dog as a specific breed. Canine enthusiasts all across Europe, and particularly in Germany, were becoming vigorously involved with the stimulating competition of dog shows. By the end of the nineteenth century, frequent dog shows were seen in Germany, with British Collies dominating the sheepdog classes.

Dog enthusiasts everywhere began looking for new and interesting breeds to enter in the rising dog sport. With a passion for their herding dogs, German sportsmen of the period were determined to prevent their dogs from becoming part of the vanishing past and made a strong effort to have the best of their herding dogs represented at the existing dog shows. A number of attempts were made to transform the wide variety of German sheepdogs into one consistent breed, or at least into one type. The first notable endeavor came with the formation of a breed club known as the Phylax Society, which formed in 1891. The club lasted only three years, splitting up in 1894 because of a heated quarrel among its members over the issue of breeding for a specific look rather than breeding for herding, driving, and protection instincts. This conflict continues to this day, causing serious debates among German Shepherd breeders and fanciers.

Six years later, on April 22, 1899, the definitive German Shepherd organization, the Verein für deutsche Schäferhunde (Society for the Promotion of the Breeding of German Shepherd Dogs), known as SV, was founded in Stuttgart (and later moved to Munich) by Ernst von Otto, Adolf Meyer (SV's first president), and Captain Max von Stephanitz, a former cavalry officer who governed the organization from 1901 to 1935. Von Stephanitz was to become the most influential force in the history and creation of the German Shepherd Dog.

From its start SV sponsored an annual championship dog show with von Stephanitz as judge for the top male. Although he was concerned with the breed's type, he was keenly interested in the qualities of intelligence and working abilities. As the primary show judge, he was able to control the breed's development. Many believe he was a breeding genius with a special gift for evaluating pedigrees and selecting dogs for their superior qualities that represented his vision of the breed. He governed his organization with an iron fist and demanded strict discipline with regard to specific breeding principles.

In its early years the SV registered all sheepdogs under very loose rules concerning appearance and origins. However, von Stephanitz regarded the dogs of some areas to be of greater importance than others. The important shepherd dog areas of Germany were considered to be Württemberg, near the Swiss Alps; Bavaria (Swabia) along the Czech border; and the central region known as Thuringia. According to statements from von Stephanitz, the Thuringian Shepherd, although smaller and wiry, was introduced for its erect ears and wolf-gray coat. The dogs from Württemberg were selected for their heavier bones, larger size, tail carriage, and other colors. The Swabian dogs were introduced for their size, strength, and gait.

The early breeders carefully selected and mated dogs with the most outstanding qualities, projecting them into one single breed. Over the years the selection process was highly focused, determined,

and disciplined. In a relatively short period of time, compared with how long it took to establish other breeds, and with the help of strict judging at dog shows, herding competitions, and ultimately obedience trials, breeders successfully developed the German Shepherd Dog as we know it today.

With full knowledge of the breed's protective instincts, von Stephanitz successfully promoted the German Shepherd Dog for police work. Hundreds of German police stations used trained dogs for public disorders and other aspects of law enforcement. Thus began the breed's reputation and great success as the ultimate Service Dog. Throughout the First World War German Shepherds were used by the military on both sides for sentry work, message running, and searching for the wounded.

Early in the history of the breed, Shepherd people quickly understood that their dogs had more to offer than herding sheep and protecting property. Because of their great intelligence, Shepherds are very willing to please, which makes them easy to train for almost anything. They are capable of performing a wide variety of jobs, making them among the most versatile of all dog breeds.

Through their successful use in the First World War, the breed developed an international reputation. They were exported to England, the United States, and most places throughout the world where serious breeding programs were developed.

In the early 1920s two very special German Shepherds appeared in motion pictures and did more to popularize the

breed than all that had been accomplished before. Strongheart and Rin-Tin-Tin were true movie stars of the silent screen and each, in his respective films, captivated the world with his endearing behavior, highly trained stunts, and feats of obvious courage. Rin-Tin-Tin was a star of such magnitude that he was responsible for the solvency of Warner Brothers Studios throughout the decade in which he lived and worked in pictures. Strongheart was equally adored, with millions of fans, and was the first dog to portray a Guide Dog for the blind.

The German Shepherd Dog has been listed among the top ten breeds registered by the American Kennel Club for decades. Their rise to this pinnacle in less than one hundred years is one of the most spectacular accomplishments in the history of purebred dogs.

CHAPTER THREE

Amazing German Shepherds

Everyone who likes dogs likes the Good Shepherd. There have never been dogs as versatile, as useful, as admired, as German Shepherds. Although they are excellent companion animals, their popularity is based on their intelligence, bravery, and loyalty. A German Shepherd is the quintessential dog. Its reputation comes from its many contributions to society and the high profile of its accomplishments. The important reason for the Shepherds' great popularity is their usefulness as Service Dogs guiding their blind partners, detecting drugs, sniffing out bombs, and searching for earthquake victims or others in need of rescue. These capabilities, in addition to the ability to participate in the various Dog Sports, make German Shepherds desirable as companion animals who, in addition to everything else, will protect you.

Few breeds are as multifaceted as German Shepherds. They are graced with a keen intelligence combined with a touching desire to please those with whom they live. Since their emergence as a breed, they have been admired and prized for their obvious skills. But there is more to the German Shepherd than herding and protection abilities. They have also excelled at conformation dog shows, field trials, tracking tests, obedience trials, dog agility tournaments, and schutzhund (protection dog) competition.

Shepherds are especially valued and cherished for their extraordinary ability to assist physically challenged human beings. The breed has become an integral part of most assistance-dog programs. They are among a handful of breeds that are used as Guide Dogs for the blind, as Service Dogs (for those in wheelchairs), as Hearing Dogs

Few breeds are as versatile as the German Shepherd.

(for the hearing impaired), and as Therapy Dogs. German Shepherds are highly desirable for this work because of their intelligence and dependability.

The Good Shepherd is also one of the finest companion animals in the world. He has succeeded far beyond the expectations of those who dared imagine such a breed back in 1899. The Good Shepherd is in many ways a public servant, an athlete, and an important member of the family. In most situations he is a loving friend and devoted partner.

Here then is a brief summary of the extensive activities in which German Shepherd Dogs are involved. It is an explanation of what makes them amazing.

Dog Shows (Conformation Shows)

There are two types of sanctioned dog shows, *Specialty* shows and *All-Breed* shows. Specialty shows are open to only one specific breed of dog or to a group of specific breeds. All-Breed shows are open to any breed, so long as it is recognized by the governing body—such as the American Kennel Club (AKC) or the United Kennel Club (UKC)—and so long as there is a sufficient number of entries to provide adequate competition.

A dog show, which is better known as a conformation show, is an amateur sports event in which dogs compete to win points in order to earn an AKC or UKC Champion title (Ch.). Once the title is earned, it appears before the dog's name in all AKC or UKC records as well as in any written reference to the dog. Becoming a champion of record is a major achievement for a dog and its owner and is not easily accomplished.

According to the American Kennel Club:

> To become an official American Kennel Club champion of record, a dog must earn fifteen points. A dog can earn from one to five points at a dog show. Wins of three, four, or five points are termed "majors." The fifteen points required for championship must be won under at least three different judges, and must include two "majors" won under different judges.

The United Kennel Club requires the following:

> *U.K.C. SHOW CHAMPION (CH.)* — Qualifications for a U.K.C. Champion: (1) must have a minimum of one hundred (100) U.K.C. points; (2) must have shown and acquired Championship points under at least three different U.K.C. licensed judges; (3) must have won two Best Males/Females under two different U.K.C. licensed judges.
>
> *U.K.C. GRAND SHOW CHAMPION (GR. CH.)* — Earned by winning: five (5) Champion of Champions show classes; in at least five (5) different U.K.C. licensed conformation shows; under at least three (3) different U.K.C. licensed judges.

Dog shows attract the largest number of participants in the Dog Sport and receive the greatest attention from the media and the general public. Conformation shows are seen on television and written about extensively in books, articles, and news stories. Among the most important AKC conformation shows in the United States are the Westminster Kennel Club Show (New York), the International Kennel Club Show (Chicago), the Santa Barbara Kennel Club Show (California), and such combined, or "cluster," shows as the River City Cluster in San Antonio. The most important UKC event is the United Kennel Club Premier (Kalamazoo, Michigan) involving two All-Breed conformation shows, combined with obedience trials, agility, specialty shows, group shows, and other competitions and demonstrations.

Conformation shows are disparaged by some as being merely beauty pageants for dogs. One may argue that there is nothing wrong with beauty pageants. Dog shows, however, are more than that. Although each dog's physical attractiveness is part of the competition at a conformation show, structure, movement, temperament, and personality are also evaluated and given equal—if not greater— importance by the show judges.

The original purpose of the conformation show was to identify those dogs that possessed a body structure and temperament most suitable for the breed's function and to select them for mating. The idea was, and still is, to improve the breed. To many spectators at a dog show, all the dogs in the ring appear to be beautiful as well as animated, and they find it difficult to guess which one is the winner. The show judge, however, considers many aspects of the dogs. His or her responsibility is to examine each dog thoroughly, compare it with the written breed standard, and determine how close it comes to the ideal, to being the *perfect* German Shepherd Dog. The dog that comes closest to the breed standard wins. There is considerable competition at a dog show and a great deal of excitement for those involved. That is why it is called the Dog Sport. The competition is intense.

The first German Shepherd Dog registered in the Stud Book of the American Kennel Club was Queen of Switzerland in 1908, when the dog was shown in New York in the Miscellaneous Group and listed as a "German Sheepdog."

In 1913 Benjamin H. Throop, of Scranton, Pennsylvania, and

Anne Tracy, of Highland Falls-on-Hudson, New York, with twenty-six other moving spirits founded the German Shepherd Dog Club of America, which was incorporated on February 7, 1916. The club's first Specialty show took place on June 11, 1915, with forty dogs benched and four points toward a Champion title. Today the club boasts more than four thousand members, with an impressive variety of activities, including committees that oversee everything from temperament to health to balancing beauty with working ability.

Every year since 1918 the German Shepherd Dog Club of America (GSDCA) hosts its National Specialty Show (known as "the National"). This is the most important competition event in the United States for serious German Shepherd Dog enthusiasts. Held in a different city each year, the National is a four-day event involving the most prestigious conformation and obedience trials for the breed. The GSDCA also honors two dog heroes, one Service Dog and one family pet, at the National. Other enjoyable events and sideshows at the National are often a "Parade of Greats," a "schutzhund exhibition," or even a "scent-hurdle race."

The object of attending this great show is to win points toward a Champion title and to garner as much reputation as possible by simply being there. The highest awards, the *Best of Breed* (BOB) and *Best of Opposite Sex* (BOS), of each National Specialty were formerly called *Grand Victor* (GV) and *Grand Victrix* (GVx). Before 1925 the designation was *Grand Champion*. For the devotee, winning anything at the National Specialty is more important, more prestigious, more precious than anything else in the competitive world involving this breed.

Over the decades the Shepherd has proven to be a consistent attraction in the show ring, setting high entry records in German Shepherd Specialty shows as well as becoming a strong contender in All-Breed shows. This is reflected by the breed's enormous AKC and UKC registration numbers. At the 1987 Westminster Dog Show, held in Madison Square Garden, 2,671 dogs in 139 breeds and varieties competed for two days in front of a panel of forty-one judges. Of all those dogs, one emerged as Best in Show, taking home the

The Westminster Dog Show in Madison Square Garden is the most prestigious AKC conformation show in the United States.

ribbons and the silver. He was Ch. Covy Tucker Hill's Manhattan, an eight-year-old German Shepherd Dog bred by Cappy Pottle and Gloria Birch, owned by Shirlee Braunstein and the late Jane A. Firestone. He was expertly handled by James A. Moses. *Manhattan* was the first German Shepherd Dog ever to win at Westminster. He will not be the last.

Anyone wishing to compete in conformation shows with a German Shepherd Dog should study the breed standard (see the Official Standard for the German Shepherd Dog in Chapter One, "Meet the German Shepherd Dog," page 27), obtain the American Kennel Club or United Kennel Club's rules and regulations for dog shows, and seek the help and advice of a breeder or an exhibitor.

Obedience Trials

An obedience trial is a sporting event in which dogs and their handlers compete for winning points that accumulate toward an obedience title. The competition takes place before a crowd of spectators and consists of specific obedience exercises in accordance with American Kennel Club or United Kennel Club rules and regulations. As the name of the sport implies, dogs and their handlers must demonstrate the ability to perform established obedience routines to a high standard and are judged by licensed AKC or UKC judges, depending on the show.

The level of difficulty of the obedience exercises is determined by the categories of competition the dog enters. The *Novice Class* tests simple, practical obedience commands used in daily living, such as Heel on Leash, Heel Free, Long Sit, and Long Down. The Novice Class offers the AKC title of *Companion Dog* (CD), proudly shown after the dog's name. The UKC Novice Class title is U-CD.

The *Open Class* consists of more demanding obedience exercises, such as Drop on Recall, Retrieve Over High Jump, and Broad Jump. Dogs entering Open Class competition must have earned a CD title from the Novice Class. The Open Class enables a dog to earn the title *Companion Dog Excellent* (CDX). The UKC Open Class title is U-CDX.

The *Utility Class* offers a high level of challenge for both dog and handler. It is a very demanding class, requiring near perfection in all exercises, some of which are Signal Exercise, Scent Discrimination, and Directed Jumping. Dogs competing in the Utility Class can earn the title *Utility Dog* (UD). Since January 1994, dogs in AKC obedience trials can earn a new title, *Utility Dog Excellent* (UDX). The UKC class title is U-UD(A or B).

In 1977 the American Kennel Club introduced its prestigious national event, the *Obedience Trial Championship*, offering the highest possible title for an obedience dog-handler team, *Obedience Trial Champion* (OTCh). Only dogs with a UD or UDX are eligible to compete. It is the only AKC obedience title placed *before* the dog's name.

German Shepherd Dogs have been outstanding in obedience competition ever since it became a licensed event. Champion Schwarzpels von Mardex was one of the first two dogs to earn all the degrees of CD, CDX, and UD under AKC rules in the early days of obedience trials, when tracking tests were included in the Utility exercises. The German Shepherd was, and still is, one of the top breeds in number of obedience titles earned.

In 1968 the German Shepherd Dog Club of America established the title of *Obedience Victor* (OV) or *Obedience Victrix* (OVx), to be awarded at its National Specialty show each year. The winning dog or bitch must win the combined scores of at least 385 points out of a possible 400; at least 190 points in Open B and Utility classes; and an AKC ribbon from a sanctioned conformation show.

Tracking Tests

Being outdoors in rugged terrain, hiking through mud and leaves, and trailing behind a German Shepherd Dog as he uses his natural scenting ability are what tracking tests have to offer the energetic dog owner. Following man-made tracks with turns of increasing difficulty and distance that are aged by time is an exercise in which your Shepherd is the leader and you are the follower. Tracking tests are totally pass-or-fail events under strict AKC guidelines for judging, and Shepherds have excelled in them.

These tests are also conducted by the United Kennel Club. Successfully completed tracking tests allow the titles *Tracking Dog* (TD) and *Tracking Dog Excellent* (TDX) to be applied after the dog's registered name in written references to him. Tracking requires a great deal of training for both dog and owner as a dog-handler team for the actual test. The tracking titles are not easily attained, and only a few dogs have earned them. The scents are laid a half hour before the test for the TD title and no less than three hours beforehand for the TDX title. The officials allow one personal item (such as a glove) at the starting place and three other personal items along the trail and at varied intervals.

German Shepherds are natural trackers; it's a skill that can be fine-tuned with training.

A dog being tested is harnessed to a twenty- to forty-foot leash held by the handler. The handler must remain at least twenty feet behind the dog. All dogs entered in the AKC tracking tests must go through a screening process that certifies them for the main event. Observing a tracking test is recommended before you attempt to become involved.

Agility Trials

An agility trial is a tournament in which individual dogs run through an obstacle course that tests their endurance, speed, and accuracy as their handlers direct them along the way. Each course must be run within a set time, which adds to the tension and excitement. With the crowd cheering the dogs on over A-frames and walls, through tunnels and weave poles, and up and down teetering seesaws, agility trials are probably the most rousing of all the dog sports and the most fun for spectators. All dogs entered in an agility trial must have speed and intelligence and have had precision training.

The agility trial was devised in England specifically for the 1978 Crufts Dog Show. It was envisioned as a minor diversion to amuse the spectators during a lull between various segments of the dog show. The event turned into a huge crowd pleaser and made a lasting impression. The pace of the demonstration was much faster than that of obedience trials and conformation judging. The enthusiasm and skill of the dogs were exciting to the audience, which responded with applause, whistles, and screams of approval. Audiences at agility events have continued to respond enthusiastically ever since.

This newest of sports for dog-and-owner competition was sure to emerge in the United States along with the popularity of fly-ball, scent hurdles, relay races, and other demonstration sports that have captured the imagination and attention of dog owners and dog lovers alike.

The sport of agility began to grow in popularity in this country after it became organized in 1986 by the United States Dog Agility Association (USDAA). This organization set standards, adopted rules, and created certified titles to be awarded for achievement in various

Agility trials test the Shepherd's intelligence, speed, and endurance.

levels of competition. There are three classes of competition: *Novice,* *Open,* and *Excellent.* With each class, the required speed increases along with the number and complexity of the obstacles. Jumps are adjusted to the size of the dogs.

Enhancing the future of agility trials in the United States is the American Kennel Club's acceptance of the sport as part of its roster of sanctioned dog events. The AKC's first licensed agility trial took place on August 11, 1995, in Houston, at the Astro World Series of Dog Shows. The event was a huge success, with 192 entries represented by 58 breeds.

Schutzhund (Clubs and Trials)

Schutz is the German word for "protection" or "defense." *Hund,* of course, means "dog." Schutzhund develops self-confidence and protection skills that should be present in working dogs, such as German Shepherds. Schutzhund clubs offer testing programs at their trials, where a dog is challenged in three areas of skill: obedience, protection, and tracking—each offered in progressive degrees of complexity. A dog may earn *Schutzhund I* (SchH I), *Schutzhund II* (SchH II), or *Schutzhund III* (SchH III) degrees. Other degrees and tests may be obtained, for those committed to the sport.

Schutzhund trials began at the turn of the twentieth century in Germany about the same time the German Shepherd Dog was being developed as a breed. Both breed development and Schutzhund standards were created and imposed by the man most responsible for the German Shepherd Dog, Max von Stephanitz. (Please see Chapter Two, "A Bit of History.")

In Germany these abilities and skills are considered to be of utmost importance for the German Shepherd Dog. The breed's governing body in Germany, Verein für deutsche Schäferhunde, or SV, demands that a Shepherd must have earned an SchH I before it may be recommended for breeding.

Schutzhund events are also conducted by the various schutzhund organizations in the United States. The largest U.S. schutzhund organization is the United Schutzhund Clubs of America, with well over 150 member clubs. The Working Dog Association (WDA), a club governed by the German Shepherd Dog Club of America, is also very involved with schutzhund activities.

Schutzhund clubs are not found in every state and must be located through German Shepherd breeders and exhibitors and various dog magazines. Although German Shepherd Dogs dominate this sport, other breeds participate, such as Doberman Pinschers, Rottweilers, Bouviers de Flandres, Giant Schnauzers, and Belgian Tervurens.

Police Dogs

The breed of choice for most canine police units is the German Shepherd Dog. Today most metropolitan police departments and sheriff's offices rely on Shepherds to track bank robbers and escaped criminals, control crowds of rioters, or find and restrain suspicious persons. Police canine units are used most often for scenting bombs, narcotics, and weapons as well as detecting evidence.

Schutzhund obedience and protection training is a challenging process.

Strong emphasis is placed on obedience and agility training before the protection skills are taught. Restraining aggressors is an important aspect of the training. A police dog is taught to attack and apprehend perpetrators if the police handler is struck or if a gun is fired. To this day more German Shepherd Dogs are used by law enforcement agencies than any other breed. With their high visibility and breed recognition, they have much to offer as a deterrent, without having to make aggressive moves against potential wrongdoers or suspects.

Dogs used for this purpose live in the homes of their police handlers as working partners and special family members. The police officers of these specialized units are completely responsible for feeding, housing, and training the dogs assigned to them. These human-dog police teams develop into completely bonded relationships, with strong ties and great caring. In most situations, the dog is greatly loved by the police officer's family as well.

Law enforcement agencies use German Shepherds more than any other breed.

Search and Rescue (SAR Dogs)

German Shepherds have dominated the field of search and rescue almost from its inception and have a high rate of success at finding lost people and disaster victims. With their strong sense of smell and their desire to please and work hard, they perform these heroic activities with reliability and devotion.

Puppies must be socialized and "sound-sure," learn to climb ladders, get into planes and helicopters, be amiable around other dogs, and be physically and mentally sound. The dogs must be trained in tracking, obedience, and agility-type courses to be prepared for the terrain they often encounter as they search for plane crash, earthquake, and disaster victims. Dog-handler teams must be in excellent physical condition in order to work long, hard hours in rugged terrain and in extreme temperatures and weather conditions. The teams consist of volunteers who search for missing persons in disasters and a German Shepherd who is scenting rather than tracking on the trail. German Shepherd Dogs figured prominently in the search for victims of the terrorist bombing at the World Trade Center in 1993 and in the Oklahoma City tragedy of 1995. A German Shepherd named Ben, whose partner was Deputy Mark Sterling, was given a Special Award from the Dog Hero of Year Awards for his heroic search-and-rescue work in Oklahoma City.

Search-and-rescue teams must be certified by the National Association of Search and Rescue (NASAR), located in Fairfax, Virginia, and are on call 24 hours a day, 365 days a year. In spite of the hard training, difficult working conditions, and tragedy encountered, no greater joy is shared than between the Shepherd, his handler, and the victim who is saved from disaster by the search-and-rescue team.

Drug and Arson Detection

Since 1970 the U.S. Customs Service has employed dogs for use in drug detection. The German Shepherd Dog, the Golden Retriever, and the Labrador Retriever are the three breeds most commonly used for this work. With an eagerness to work and a keen scenting ability, they are well suited for this work. Through extensive reward training, the dogs are employed to sniff out narcotics at airports, maritime facilities, and post offices—resulting in thousands of drug seizures, with the street value running in the hundreds of millions of dollars.

Arson Dogs have been known to detect fire-causing agents in amounts so infinitesimal that not even forensic laboratories could identify them. These fire-sniffing dogs are given reward training similar to that of Drug Detection Dogs and are taught to signal their handlers when they find what they are after. With their highly developed scenting ability, Arson Dogs are trained to sniff out and signal that they have found materials with fire-causing accelerants, no matter how obscurely located—under water, ice, or piles of debris. The Arson Dog's purpose is to help fire marshals figure out how or what started a fire. The dogs' findings reveal whether a fire was started deliberately and make an important contribution to finding the culprit.

In addition to a keen scenting capability for their work, German Shepherd Drug and Arson Dogs must be in top physical condition. To prepare them for real-life situations in building searches, they are trained regularly on an obstacle course that consists of hurdles (such as picket and solid fences, shrubs, open windows) and broad jumps. They must crawl through tubes that simulate tunnels; balance themselves on catwalks that are like fire escapes; and scramble through low, flat crawl spaces and rubble that resemble explosion or earthquake sites. The dogs are also taught how to search a building so they can flush one out prior to officers' entering a potentially dangerous situation.

Therapy Dogs

Many German Shepherd Dogs are informally referred to as *Therapy Dogs* because their owners regularly take them to visit patients in hospitals, nursing homes, and other medical facilities, where they give their love and affection to everyone. Most health-care providers believe in the medical benefits of bringing together emotionally hurting humans and dogs, whose boundless affection and unconditional acceptance are capable of breaching many emotional and psychological barriers.

German Shepherd Dogs enjoy this activity and benefit from it, too, because it gives them an opportunity to express their highly social behavior and love of people. When Shepherds come to visit, they brighten the lives of patients in hospitals, nursing homes, and old-age homes, as well as the physically challenged, psychiatric patients, abused children, and those in prison rehabilitation programs. Therapy Dogs perform their magic by making direct emotional contact with everyone and anyone, no strings attached.

Since 1977 the Delta Society has fostered the concept of nurturing contact between humans and animals. The society is the leading international information clearinghouse and action center for the interaction of people, animals, and the environment and for animal-assisted therapy. This organization's studies on the effects of animals on human health have been the inspiration for German Shepherd Dog owners' generous therapy visits.

The German Shepherd Dog's even temperament and gentle, loving personality have made it one of the most welcome breeds in hospitals across the country. Shepherds are also likely to spend much time with disturbed or depressed adults and relate equally to the outgoing and talkative, the severely depressed, and even the abusive patient. Their generous expression of affection for everyone always evokes a friendly, happy response.

Patients who never talk to anyone will suddenly talk to a Shepherd and his handler, will stroke the dog's coat, and will perhaps become nostalgic about dogs they have known and loved—which may lead to other personal discussions. Some patients never say a word to anyone but allow a dog to lay his head on their lap and look up as they stare at each other. Such patients are often drawn out of their depression and talk to the medical staff later, the topic of conversation being the dog that came to call.

Hospitalized children with emotional problems can be the most difficult for visiting dogs. Many such children are aggressive or hyperactive or completely withdrawn. They can be very rough and must be prevented from being abusive to the dogs. Fortunately, German Shepherd Dogs have a high tolerance for such behavior, even if it involves pushing, pulling, and screeching. Encouraging such children to comb and brush the dogs or simply talk to them often elicits a calmed, gentle response, depending on their mood and the severity of their problems. Through it all, Shepherds smile, wag, and tolerate most unruly behavior from young patients. The children often find touching ways to say thank you to the dogs for being their friends, sometimes with a hug, sometimes with a handmade Christmas card.

Service Dogs

A Service Dog has been trained to work with physically disabled people. These remarkable dogs are always with their partners and perform such important tasks as pulling wheelchairs, manipulating simple household appliances, turning lights on and off, opening cupboard doors, and retrieving out-of-reach or dropped items. These seemingly simple chores assume enormous importance to the partner. Dogs help them enjoy greater independence in most aspects of their lives. Service Dogs make it possible for their partners to go to school, get a job, travel, and, in general, enjoy a full life.

The concept of the Service Dog was created by Dr. Bonita M. Bergin, who as a young woman traveled abroad working as a teacher. The idea came to her while teaching in Australia and traveling throughout Asia and Europe, where she discovered that disabled people in other countries were more self-reliant and independent by necessity. She observed that many of them used donkeys and other manageable pack animals for assistance.

In the mid-1970s Bergin returned to the United States and eventually developed the idea of training dogs to assist physically impaired people. By the early 1980s, after several years of struggle and sacrifice, she had structured a basic program for acquiring specific dogs, training them, and making them available to those willing to try them out. She incorporated and named her infant organization

Canine Companions for Independence (CCI). This remarkable operation has grown over the years as a major force for good throughout the United States, with branches in a number of metropolitan areas. She established rapport with other assistance-dog organizations and founded Assistance Dogs International, an amalgam of similar training programs inviting membership from other countries.

Service Dogs are trained to assist those with physical disabilities, particularly those who use wheelchairs. Another category of assistance dogs provided by CCI is the Hearing Dog. Hearing Dogs are for people who are deaf and hard of hearing. These dogs alert their human partners to such crucial sounds as doorbells, telephones, alarm clocks, smoke alarms, and crying children. Although German Shepherd Dogs can function as Hearing Dogs, only a few are selected for that service.

A great number of Service Dogs are German Shepherd Dogs. Other breeds utilized are Golden Retrievers, Labrador Retrievers, Border Collies, and Pembroke Welsh Corgis.

Guide Dogs for People Who Are Blind

The German Shepherd Dog who guides his blind partner is described as kind of heart, friendly, intelligent, with no sign of fear or aggression, sensitive, and dedicated to duty. The three breeds most commonly used as Guide Dogs are Labrador Retrievers, Golden Retrievers, and German Shepherd Dogs. As one of the three breeds used by Guide Dog institutions, the German Shepherd Dog is chosen for its size, coat, temperament, and willingness to work. Puppies are raised in volunteer homes to socialize them and familiarize them with most situations. They are returned to their respective schools between the ages of twelve and eighteen months to begin rigorous training and testing. Only the best will be chosen for three to six months of additional training and extensive hard work and will then be matched with a blind partner. The dog-human team are then given on-premises training and situational work in busy traffic and on public transportation.

The pioneering Guide Dog school in the United States, the Seeing Eye, in Morristown, New Jersey, was established in 1929. It was inspired by earlier work with blinded veterans done in Germany after the First World War. Buddy, a German Shepherd Dog, and her blind partner, Morris Frank, a founder of the Seeing Eye, trained in Switzerland and came back to the United States, where Frank publicized the advantages of working with a Guide Dog. Currently there are fourteen active programs functioning in the United States and three in Canada.

The dogs are given to the blind partner at no charge. This is made possible by donations from many concerned people

German Shepherds' temperament and willingness to work help make them excellent Guide Dogs.

upon whom all existing schools and programs depend. Guide dogs, among which is the German Shepherd, have been so successful at giving newfound independence to their blind teammates that a New York couple, Ed and Toni Eames, now relocated in Fresno, California, have become the first blind obedience handlers to train their Guide Dogs (Golden Retrievers) to American Kennel Club CD and CDX titles and Bermudan CDs. They write a feature column for *Dog World* magazine, the title of which clearly describes their relationship with their guides, "Partners in Independence."

The Eameses are the authors of the book *A Guide To Guide Dog Schools* and team-teach workshops and seminars dealing with disability issues for teachers, veterinarians, and others interested in the subject. Toni Eames has a master's degree in rehabilitation counseling from Hunter College. Ed Eames has a Ph.D. from Cornell University and is a retired professor of anthropology from Temple University and Baruch College.

The Eameses believe that the goal of giving independence to a blind person is achieved when a dog-human team have the freedom and ability to travel in comfort and safety. In their book they state:

> Approximately 8,000 guide dog teams are presently working in Canada and the United States. Since there is an estimated population of 750,000 blind and visually impaired people in these countries, it means fewer than 1.5% of them use guide dogs as their basic means of mobility. One reason for this low percentage, we believe, is lack of information about these remarkable canine assistants. Our goal is to fill this information gap.

To order their book *A Guide to Guide Dog Schools*, send $10 to: Ed and Toni Eames, 3376 N. Wishon, Fresno, CA 93704-4832. Make checks payable to Disabled on the Go (D.O.G.). See the Appendix for a listing of Guide Dog schools.

Dogs in Movies and TV

On October 17, 1917, a German Shepherd puppy named Edzel von Oeringen was whelped in Germany, where he trained for police work as a young dog. In 1920 he was sold and exported to White Plains, New York. He went to live with a writer for the silent screen, Jane Murfin, and her husband, director Larry Trimble. They changed the dog's name to Strongheart, who became the first dog hero in motion pictures. The rest is history. Thus began the German Shepherd's long reign in movies as the ultimate hero and companion. His first film, *The Silent Call*, was in 1921. From the start, Strongheart became a major movie star with an international following. The dog starred in several other pictures; in one, he portrayed a Guide

Dog for a blind person. Sadly, he died prematurely, ending his short but spectacular career.

The immortal Rin-Tin-Tin was the second dog to become a major movie star. He, too, was a German Shepherd Dog who had an enormous impact on audiences everywhere. His first film was *Where the North Begins* in 1923.

Rinty's owner, Lee Duncan, an American airman in the First World War, found the dog in 1918 and rescued him as a puppy from a deserted German trench in France. He named the little dog Rin-Tin-Tin after a good-luck charm, a small doll, that was popular with French soldiers at the time. His tender feelings for the dog compelled him to bring him to California, where fate and good luck smiled upon the man and his dog. Rin-Tin-Tin appeared in more than forty films over a nine-year span and earned over a million dollars for his owner. His popularity was so great that he received ten thousand fan letters a week. He was an important part of the reason for Warner Brothers' solvency. In 1932 he died, leaving behind offspring who became his successors in motion pictures and then television. Rin-Tin-Tin was the most famous German Shepherd of all time.

German Shepherds continued to grace the silver screen with Roy Rogers and Dale Evans's Bullet, as much a partner in the movies and TV series as their famous horse, Trigger.

In recent years the German Shepherd Dog has maintained a high profile by starring in such movies as *K-9* with James Belushi, Walt Disney's *Chips, the War Dog,* Brian DePalma's *Body Double,* and The Family Channel's production of *Rin-Tin-Tin, Canine Cop.* Obviously, the German Shepherd Dog's place in movies and television is secure and here to stay.

German Shepherd Dogs are truly amazing.

CHAPTER FOUR

The Shepherd Bond

The Right Way to Love Your Puppy

Bonding is simply the creation of a strong emotional connection based on a growing relationship. When people do not bond with their dogs, they find it harder to train them, harder to control them, harder to enjoy them, but, unfortunately, easier to part with them. When a German Shepherd Dog first comes into your home, bonding with him is the first thing you should accomplish, even before training. Bonding with your dog is the most important thing you can do.

Everyone loves a puppy. The first time he enters his home as a frisky, uninhibited youngster, his new family finds his energy, curiosity, and comical mischief exhilarating. Despite the little dog's howling through the first night or two and his confusion as to where to relieve himself, everyone enjoys playing with him. This interlude of good feeling, unfortunately, may not last. Puppies grow up, and many new dog owners, having never considered what their adorable canine babies might be like as adult dogs, are surprised by the great differences in size, looks, and behavior. Living with a dog requires accepting him in the various stages of his life. The delightful antics and cute looks of a puppy inevitably come to an end; change is the only constant factor.

Sustaining love for a pet throughout his lifetime requires the creation of an emotional bond that holds the dog and his family together in a happy, satisfying relationship. If the value of creating a bond is understood, a pet dog will always be loved and cared for, especially in old age.

A puppy's new family is always exhilarated by his energy, curiosity, and comical mischief.

Puppy characteristics are eventually replaced by the endearing qualities of grown dogs, such as their love and devotion for those they live with, their participation in everyday family life, and the attention and companionship they lavishly give. Adult Shepherds are much more interesting than puppies. As grown-ups they are athletes who become seriously involved with your family and enjoy playing with you or doing anything else you want—as long as it is with you. Full-grown Shepherds are happiest when they are with you. They relate to their family members in meaningful ways, not the least of which is guarding and protecting them. They are very caring animals.

Like most dogs, German Shepherds have no difficulty bonding with all family members, and they do it in a matter of minutes. It is in their nature. Once the bond is established, it remains for a lifetime unless a dog is abused or neglected.

Not all dog owners, however, bond with their pets. Many are simply not aware of the concept, its importance, its benefits, or how to do it, despite the fact that bonding is as natural for people as it is for dogs.

How to Bond with Your German Shepherd Dog

Creating an emotional bond with a dog involves generous expressions of love and affection, talk, socializing, play, and training.

Love and affection as a bonding technique. Shepherd puppies are irresistible; if you come within six feet of one, you cannot escape the urge to hold it, hug it, and play with it. The desire to express your feelings so openly is good for the pup, good for you, and good for both of you together. That desire is the essence of bonding. Long after puppyhood the shared feelings will remain through good times and bad. A German Shepherd will respond appropriately to your moods and inner feelings. It is this quality that brings them closer to their owners. Becoming close with your dog is the goal of bonding.

Freely expressing your affection not only cultivates your dog's personality but also creates a strong, unbreakable bond and then

Bonding makes your German Shepherd a part of the family.

keeps reinforcing it on a daily basis. A puppy left alone in the yard will still love its owner. Shepherds are like that. Leaving the dog out of your activities, however, fails to establish the bond that makes him a member of the family and an important part of your life.

German Shepherds love their families unconditionally, *just because they exist.* If you raise a pup with the idea that he is loved and wanted, he will always be at his best when you teach him something. He will always be a "good dog." Puppies are innocent. They do not chew the rug or pee on the floor on purpose. All they want is to eat, play, and be loved by the people in their lives who are their leaders.

If you never place your dog in a situation in which he fails or is bad, he will always consider himself a great dog living a happy life. This is a matter of owner attitude and behavior. A supportive, approving attitude encourages a puppy to grow into a dog with self-confidence, to love and trust you, to work with you, and to accept your leadership role in his life. Most important, it establishes and deepens the bond between you and your dog. Love and affection are the very essence of a bond between a dog and his family.

Talking to your dog as a bonding technique. Talk to your dog. If you do, your puppy or adult dog will always run to you with enthusiasm at the sound of your voice. Never yell or allow your voice to show anger or hysteria. This is important even if you are reprimanding your pet. In dog training a voice correction requires a firm but *controlled* tone of voice in two- or three-word sentences. (See Corrections in Chapter Eight, "Obedience-Training Your German Shepherd.")

German Shepherds are sensitive and respond to your tone of voice and body language more than to harsh reprimands you bellow out. Sometimes direct eye contact and a stiff posture are all that is needed to indicate your displeasure with your dog's behavior.

While your dog is still a puppy, try talking to him in a high-pitched tone of voice because it sounds pleasant and is not threatening. Talk to him about everything while hugging him, kissing him, and touching him. Much as a human mother and father cootchy-coo their baby in a high-pitched, soft voice, don't hesitate to do so with a German Shepherd puppy. The words aren't important, other than the repetition of his new name. It's the tone of your voice and the feelings behind it that count.

When you talk to your dog, punctuate your conversations by accentuating key words in your speech along with happy-sounding variations in your tone of voice. Explain things and ask questions; it will strengthen the bond.

Do not holler at your dog. If he makes you angry, the most effective reprimand is to ignore him. Many breeds cannot stand being ignored and immediately want to make up and please you. For the purpose of bonding, talk to your dog in a kind, gentle, affectionate way. And do it often.

Touching your dog as a part of bonding. Touch is a major part of bonding. Touch him on his eyes, his nose, his feet, and his back. Talking to your dog while touching him deepens the bond because it communicates your feelings for him. Your dog will always want to be with you. Talk to your puppy as you would talk to a child. Even though your dog won't understand exactly what you are saying, he will understand your feelings for him.

When your dog is still small, you can pick him up with two hands and hold him close to you by supporting his front and rear ends equally and cradling him next to your body. Never pick up your puppy by the front or rear legs only. Do not use a one-hand-under-the-stomach method, either. If the puppy struggles, he could fall and injure himself. Once he's too large to pick up, come down to his level for hugs and kisses. It is unwise to encourage your young pup to jump up on you for affection—unless you are prepared to deal with eighty pounds slamming into you or your friends when your adult Shepherd is in the mood for affection.

Socializing as a bonding technique. Dog behaviorists and professional trainers have proven that a puppy's personality is shaped or imprinted most dramatically during the seventh to sixteenth weeks. Positive and negative experiences leave lasting impressions on your pup that will affect him in adulthood. For example, a puppy that never leaves his quiet house or yard during this period will react fearfully to street traffic at eight months of age. Therefore, it is your responsibility to get him out into the world and expose him to new people and situations at an early age.

Many breeders discourage new owners from taking puppies outside the home until vaccinations are complete, which in some cases can be as late as four months. While this concern is justified, a com-

Your new puppy should be exposed to as many people as possible.

promise can be reached. Avoid allowing your puppy to play with other dogs for now. Once his shots are completed, he can be socialized with other safe dogs. This is highly recommended so that he learns to coexist peacefully with his own kind. Young dogs who are unsocialized with others and living with only their human family can become aggressive as adults when meeting other dogs. You should also avoid taking your puppy to one of the so-called dog parks or any other situation in which large numbers of dogs congregate. Viruses can be transmitted easily by contact to an incompletely protected puppy, even from an apparently healthy carrier dog. Parasitic eggs can live in scooped grass or dirt, infecting your puppy and contaminating your own yard when your puppy defecates.

Your new Shepherd puppy should be exposed to as many people, noises, places, and situations as possible soon after his vaccinations are effective. Allow him to socialize with other people and other dogs, *where practical.* Take him everywhere in your car: on short trips to shops, to the car wash, on social visits with your friends—wherever you can. Everybody wants to pet a puppy. Being petted socializes your dog and gets him accustomed to new people and places. This has a profound influence on the developing bond between you. He will very much appreciate your taking him places. If you have more than one dog, this will be a special time for him to be with you exclusively. Socializing is an important aspect of bonding.

Your German Shepherd Dog should never become a so-called one-man dog. He should love everyone and everything without diminishing his feelings for you, his teacher and best friend. It is safer and more pleasant for your dog to welcome everyone who comes to your home, provided that they behave themselves. Although the adult Shepherd should announce the presence of a stranger, serving as a deterrent against trouble, he should not threaten anyone who enters your home unless that person indicates trouble.

The flip side of socializing is teaching your puppy to stay alone. This should start the day he comes to live with you. Place him in his crate and allow him to lie quietly as you leave the room. It will not be a big deal if you do not make it one. Come and go matter-of-factly with no hugs or overly enthusiastic talk. Do not gush or make guilt-ridden promises. Do not build up your dog's expectations when you leave with statements about coming back *reeeaal soon!*

Similarly, do not make a big emotional production of your return. Doing so only serves to create anxiety and restlessness about being left alone. On your return do not tell the dog what a good boy he was. Do not crate him immediately before leaving and do not release him the minute you return. Maintain a casual air. Simply open the crate door when it is convenient and go about your business. Playtime can come shortly afterward. However, if your puppy is on a housebreaking schedule, do not release him in the house until he has had an opportunity to relieve himself outside.

During the first week with your new dog, make several short, unscheduled trips to the store or around the block. Come and go at irregularly timed intervals, alternately using the front and back doors. When you return, resume some household chore before releasing the puppy from his crate.

Socializing your dog properly and not creating separation anxiety develops the best possible bond between you and your pet.

The other dog. Having another dog can possibly hinder the development of the bond between your new puppy and the family if you keep the puppy and the other dog together most of the time. Because all dogs are more likely to be drawn to each other, your new puppy may not bond with you or those living with you. Make it a rule to keep your new puppy with the *people* in your family about four to six hours a day. At night allow the puppy to sleep by himself, in a crate, if possible.

If you want your new dog to bond with you and your family, give the puppy this quality time with the family for at least a month. Otherwise, the youngster's sociability will never develop and he will become shy or aggressive. Bonding must take place between your new puppy and your entire family. It is a very important aspect of living with a pet. Do not allow the dogs in your house to bond with each other and not with everyone else.

Play as a bonding technique. German Shepherd puppies are like most puppies: they like to play. They will play with you, other people, or other dogs, if given the chance. If there is no one to play with, they will amuse themselves with solitary games.

They love to walk, hike, retrieve a stick, or do anything else you want to do with them. Games of retrieval with a ball or Frisbee are very pleasurable because running after things is natural behavior for them. Running after a ball, of course, is good exercise and great fun for the German Shepherd Dog.

Probably the number-one favorite toy of German Shepherds is the Kong toy, which is virtually indestructible. Not only will your Shepherd chase and retrieve this bouncing, unpredictable toy, he will enjoy dropping and chasing it when you are not there to throw it to him. Its very hard rubber construction is resistant to both the sharp teeth of puppies and the strong jaws of adult Shepherds. A large Kong toy is surely a long-lasting investment.

Other suitable toys are cressite or hard rubber balls. The ball should be large enough to prohibit the puppy's swallowing it by accident. Balls should never be tossed in the air to be caught, as they are very hard and could crack a tooth or scare a young puppy on impact. Tennis balls should never be left with pups, who could skin or chew them into pieces that could be swallowed. Rubber or cloth tug toys encourage your puppy to play tug-of-war. Never apply extreme resistance against your puppy's front teeth. This could alter his bite and affect the alignment of his teeth and jaw.

At no time should you allow the puppy's enthusiasm to get out of control. Any overt signs of aggression or attempts to snap at or bite your hand should not be tolerated. Good sense should tell you when the dog is no longer playing a game. You must be able to end it without a fight and when you choose. If you feel that your puppy's behavior with a tug toy is beyond play and perhaps too aggressive, remove the toy until you get advice from your breeder or from a professional trainer.

German Shepherds love hide-and-seek games and, because of their intelligence, are capable of building a large vocabulary. By naming different objects or toys, you can easily teach your Shepherd to find things that you have hidden. This is a game that will provide years of fun for you both and can come in handy if you choose to enter tracking tests or if you simply misplace your keys.

Games that you should avoid with your puppy are ones that cause him to become boisterous or allow dominant behavior on his part. Pushing, shoving, or slapping games may start as fun and turn ugly when your puppy starts using his teeth. Your next response to being nipped or bitten may be to smack your puppy, which in turn will cause fear and resentment. These games — usually, but not always, played with puppies by male owners — are unacceptable and unproductive. Ask yourself why you would ever want to encourage your best friend to use his teeth on you. And if he needs to protect you in the future against a robber or mugger, do you want him to back down because he's afraid of being hit?

Of great interest to people and dogs are conformation dog shows, obedience trials, tracking tests, the sport of agility (competitive obstacle courses), and fly-ball (relay races with a caught ball), which are all activities that German Shepherds have excelled in. Do not lose sight of the reason for the involvement: to have fun with your dog and help develop the bond. If you keep that in mind, the competition will always be play activity, and you are always the winner because you have each other. You can't lose that way.

Training as a bonding technique. Dog training is essential for creating an adaptive pet that must survive in a human environment. However, an important side benefit is bonding.

When you obedience-train your dog, you develop the ability to control him. The process for doing this involves close, personal contact and direct communication between you and the dog. These are the essential ingredients for creating the emotional bond that is so necessary for a lasting relationship.

When training your dog in the proper way, which is to say using the motivational techniques of rewards and corrections, you must communicate on a meaningful level. You are required to convey to the dog your approval when he does the right thing and your disapproval when he does the wrong thing.

When you train your dog, you teach him to obey various commands that he must perform in a precise manner. The teaching process involves talking, touching, socializing, and, in a sense, playing. Whenever the dog does the right thing, he is lavishly praised and given a great deal of encouragement. When he does not obey, he is given a correction, which may be a tug of the leash or a firm verbal reprimand. Both aspects of training involve communication; that is how bonding is accomplished. Even when housebreaking your dog, you are instructed to make a big fuss over him when he relieves himself in the right place. He must be walked and given his food and water on a frequent schedule. He must be confined to one area. He must be corrected for mistakes. These are all close-contact activities that create an involvement between the dog and his family. These, too, set the bond.

Other ways of bonding with your dog. Whatever mischief your puppy gets into that makes you laugh, such as going into the bathroom and stealing toilet paper, can be turned around as part of the bonding process.

You can bond with your dog by talking to him as you feed him. "Hey, here comes dinner. Here's chow, puppy." The puppy will gaze at you as you communicate.

You can bond with your dog when you're medicating him with eye drops or ear drops by trying to make it fun or by soothing his anxiety. You can bond when you groom him. Every time you touch him, you can talk to him and make it a happy occasion. Massaging your dog creates a feeling of relaxation for both of you as well as a feeling of physical communication.

Bear in mind that a puppy is mischievous, gets into trouble, and makes annoying mistakes. He does everything wrong. He chews. He nips. He jumps. He digs. He mouths. And he can be a pain in the you-know-what. If you get angry at the little dog and yell at him, he

will become frightened even though his behavior was normal. This fear destroys the bond before it even has a chance to develop. What could be more important than your puppy wanting your love, affection, and attention? That need overshadows "Oh, my god, he just went to the bathroom on the floor." When you think of bonding, think about your dog as a baby and you as his parent. Consider him to be a student who needs your teaching, not your anger.

Puppies have the same needs as babies. They need love, food, and nurturing. You cannot love them too much. You cannot be too good to them. To bond with your dog is to learn how to love him. Dogs that are bonded with their families usually have a strong desire to please them.

A new dog, young or old, must feel that he belongs, that he is a part of the family. Once this is accomplished, his desire to become part of the family is strong, and the bond between you is in place.

◆ ◆ ◆

Shepherd Gear
(What Your Dog Needs)

To make the newest member of your family content and secure, you'll need some Shepherd gear. Shortly after your new dog scurries through the door and sniffs around the house for the first time, he is going to look for something to drink, something to eat, and a place to pee. Then he will introduce himself to everybody, explore his new domain, and express his curiosity about his new home and family. After all that, you can be sure he will look for a comfortable corner to curl up in and sleep for a while, a place he can call his own.

In the beginning, your goal should be to convince your dog gently that this is now his home; that he is wanted, appreciated, and loved; and that everything is right with the world. You can easily accomplish this end with good handling, patience and understanding, and the right dog equipment and supplies. A puppy's material needs are not extensive. Some things are pure luxury, and others are quite necessary. If you want to start him off on the right paw, you should have on hand the following recommended Shepherd gear *before the dog arrives.*

A Wire Dog Crate

A wire crate (or *dog crate*) is a collapsible cage made of thick metal wire with a solid metal floor (coated pan) and a hinged door at the front. Some crates also open from the top as an added safety feature, while others come with a slanted front, making them easier to fit into the back of a station wagon. A wire crate is an important investment for a new dog owner because it can be used in a number of valuable ways for the life of the dog. It is useful for confinement when housebreaking, solving behavior problems, and preventing a dog from getting into trouble when he cannot be supervised. The crate also functions as an indoor doghouse, a place of his own, allowing the dog free access when the wire door is kept open. Once the crate is no longer needed to confine the dog, it becomes a sanctuary, a safety area, a place to rest and get away from it all. The wire crate becomes the core area of your dog's territory almost immediately after it is introduced to him.

If you are going to drive your new dog home in the family car, it is advisable to get a wire crate beforehand so that you can transport your dog in safety and comfort. Although it is tempting to hold the puppy in your lap (as someone else drives), placing him in a wire crate is safer. A puppy's bones are soft and easily broken or dislocated if he flies out of your lap during a sudden stop or collision. The dog is less likely to be injured if he is in his crate. Spread a large towel on the bottom of the crate for traction, place the dog inside, close the wire door, and drive away. In the event the puppy has his own "accident," it is easier to clean up the crate than the seat of the car. Leaving his previous home and adjusting to his first car ride is likely to upset his stomach, causing him to throw up or go to the toilet. Take a roll of paper towels and a large plastic bag with you.

Wire crates can be bought at many pet supply stores and in all pet supply catalogs. When selecting a crate, consider the current size of your Shepherd puppy and the full size he will grow to be. The crate you buy should allow your dog to sit up without hitting his head on the top and to lie down, stretched out completely. Start out with a crate that is slightly smaller than what he will need as an adult dog. Once the dog is fully grown, get one that is big enough for an adult German Shepherd Dog. It is more comforting for the dog if the inside is cozy and provides just a bit more room than his body needs. If there is too much interior space, the crate loses its den-like quality. An alternative to buying two different-size crates is to get one that is adult size and reduce the unneeded space by placing a wire crate divider where needed inside (fixed to the sides of the crate), like a temporary wall. Such dividers can be purchased. Leave just enough room for the dog to lie down or sit up. As the weeks and months pass, keep moving the partition back as needed until the puppy grows into a full-size dog (approximately one year).

High-pile imitation lambskin pads spread across the bottom pan make the crate soft and cozy, making it very appealing to the dog. Considering the comfort offered by a crate, it is not unusual for a dog to go to his crate on his own. If you own more than one dog, they may both curl up together. A good wire crate (along with an exercise pen and a puppy gate) is a good investment in your dog's health and happiness. Therefore, it is recommended that you buy one of high quality that will last for years. A good crate should collapse for traveling ease and provide comfort for your dog. Newer epoxy crates offer beautiful designer colors to blend in with home decor. Remember, a sturdy dog crate helps to avoid chewed carpets and furniture and gives the dog owner peace of mind. A wire crate is a wise, considerate, humane piece of equipment when used properly and is extremely effective and useful. Other important uses for crates and how to employ them can be found in chapters on housebreaking, obedience training, behavior problems, and bonding.

Super Bowls

Buying food and water bowls for your dog is not a simple matter. Catalogs and pet supply shops, especially the huge pet supply stores found in shopping malls, offer an incredible array of types, sizes, shapes, and materials. There may be more bowls to choose from than types of food to put in them. However, it helps to understand that various bowl types function in different and useful ways.

Shape. The first consideration should be the shape of the bowl. Some bowls are wide at the bottom and narrow at the top and usually deeper than the average bowl. They are meant to be used by dogs with long, hanging ears. Bowls of this shape prevent the ears from sloshing in the bowl while allowing the dog to get at the food or water. Adult German Shepherds have erect, moderately pointed ears and do not require this type of bowl, although one can be used. Also available are puppy pans that feature a raised center, leaving a circular channel around the outside, allowing more than one puppy to feed at the same time. Shepherds should have their food and water given to them in conventional bowls with straight or slightly slanted sides and flat bottoms. If the dog is going to be fed on a smooth or slippery surface, such as linoleum, get a bowl with a rubber ring on the bottom to prevent it from sliding back and forth. Some bowls are heavily weighted on the bottom to discourage the dog from tipping them over.

Size. The average adult German Shepherd needs a two-quart bowl; larger dogs require a three-quart bowl. The capacity of the bowl depends on the size of your dog, his appetite, and whether you live with more than one dog.

Twin elevated feeders are bowls that sit together in a sturdy metal rack so that they never touch the floor. These bowls can be obtained in various sizes and heights. They make it easier for a fully grown dog to eat, although you can achieve the same effect by placing conventional bowls on a stack of cinder blocks or on a milk crate. Elevated feeders prevent dogs from eating off the ground and avoid a lot of bending for dogs and pet owners. Raising your dog's food bowl may help prevent the life-threatening condition known as *bloat*. See Chapter Twelve, "Medical Problems Common to the German Shepherd Dog," Gastric Dilation-Volvulus (bloat). Some breeders and dog show people believe food and water bowls should not be placed lower than the dogs' shoulders in order to develop and maintain good posture and a dignified presence.

Shallow bowls are made for smaller dogs (they hold less food), and deeper bowls are for larger dogs (they hold more food). There are large, plastic, self-feeding bins that store large quantities of dry food and dispense a little at a time. Every time the dog eats, more food drops into the bottom tray. These bowls enable dogs to eat whenever they are hungry. You can also buy large and small motorized food containers that work with a timer, serving a measured amount of food at designated times.

Bowl materials. Most dog breeders agree that the best food and water bowls are made of stainless steel or stoneware. If you purchase a ceramic bowl, avoid those that were fired in the manufacturing process with a lead-based glaze, as they can lead to medical problems. Do not buy thin-gauge metal or plastic bowls, which can be chewed through quite easily, creating injuries if pieces are swallowed. Thick, hard plastic bowls of high quality are acceptable, though not as durable as stainless steel. Some breeders believe that plastic bowls can actually change the color of a dog's nose. Some breeders use large stainless-steel buckets for water or for carrying large quantities of dog food. These are practical, efficient, and easy to keep clean.

A Dog Bed

All puppies should have a cozy bed to sleep on. You can help a puppy leaving its mother and litter mates get over the bewildering change in its life with a warm, soft bed, which will serve as a substitute for the comfort of the nest.

Although nothing can truly replace the beat of his mother's heart or the reassurance of her breathing, a soft dog bed helps your puppy a great deal. If he came from a source other than a kennel, where he curled up with other dogs, he has slept on shredded paper or cedar chips with or without other puppies not related to him, and a bed of his own will be an appreciated change. Either way, a comfortable dog bed will help the newest member of your family make an easier adjustment to his home.

A blanket or a large towel placed in a corner of the room is adequate. These can be washed easily, and it will not create a hardship for anyone if they are chewed up. For a more pleasing appearance, pillow-like, basket-type, and doghouse-type dog beds are sold in pet supply stores and mail-order catalogs. They come in a wide variety of prices, types, and levels of luxury. All of them are satisfactory. You will never hear a world of complaint from your dog.

In addition to dog beds, you can also find manufactured dog blan-

kets designed to resist the digging, chewing, and soiling behavior of puppies; acrylic fake-fur pet beds in various sizes and shapes; dog pillows with washable covers; padded or inflated floor mats that are lightweight and easy to pack in a suitcase; and orthopedic dog beds and travel beds that fit into the backseat of a car and attach to the seat belt. Some dog beds fit comfortably inside a wire dog crate, especially the pillow type. However, do not use a pillow inside a crate for a puppy during housebreaking. A puppy just might chew the stuffing out of a pillow and swallow the material.

It is worth noting that in warm weather a German Shepherd prefers the cool surface of the floor or the smooth bottom of his wire crate. Older, arthritic dogs appreciate a large dog basket with a soft cushion in it, especially in cold weather.

Puppygate

Puppygate has nothing to do with political scandal. It is about keeping your dog out of trouble. Most dog trainers correctly advise their clients not to allow a puppy or untrained dog to have the run of the house when his family is too busy to watch him or when no one is home. An untrained puppy is certain to leave a mess to clean up after he relieves himself everywhere (they love carpets) in addition to getting into all kinds of trouble, such as chewing the furniture and whatever else he can sink his teeth into. *Confining a dog is an important aspect of housebreaking.* It is impossible to train most puppies to control themselves if they are *not* confined to one small area. A puppy gate does the job. See Chapter Seven, "Housebreaking Your German Shepherd Dog."

Confining your pet to one room and closing the door isolates him—and isolation is an unnatural condition for all dogs. He will become bewildered, upset, lonely, and bored. A dog's response to being shut away is to bark, howl, and whine. In extreme cases isolation brings on *separation anxiety,* an abnormal fear of being left alone that can involve frantic attempts to escape: chewing the bottom out of the door, clawing the walls, excessive elimination, all in addition to barking, howling, and whining. Do not isolate your dog. There is a better way.

Confining your puppy to a familiar room, such as the kitchen, is a healthier, happier solution and almost always avoids unpleasant behavior. Simply block the doorway with a puppy gate. It allows the dog to watch everything that goes on in the other rooms and not feel isolated, even if no one is home. With the door to the room open and the gate attached, your puppy is able to see into the other rooms and feel less confined. Puppy (or child) gates are sold in hardware stores, pet supply stores, and mail order catalogs for pet owners. Highly recommended gates are those that come in plastic-covered wood. Most of them work with a spring mechanism that applies pressure to each side of the doorway. Pet supply catalogs stock them in extra-wide sizes for special situations. Avoid accordion-type gates. As your Shepherd grows, you will need two gates, one placed on top of the other, to prevent your dog from jumping over.

Collars

Puppies. Buy a soft, adjustable buckle or snap-together collar made of nylon, leather, or rolled leather. Experienced dog owners get inexpensive puppy collars at first because they must be replaced several times as the dog grows. Check it daily for proper fit. There should be enough room for two fingers to slip in and out easily between the collar and your puppy's neck. It must not be too tight or too loose. *Attach an ID tag or one of the many ID products available to the collar, with your home and work telephone numbers etched on it. If your dog gets away from you, a proper ID could help get him back and even save his life.*

Adult dogs. For everyday use, a simple, buckle collar made of nylon or cotton webbing with an ID tag attached is recommended. Some German Shepherd breeders suggest nylon collars with a safety-release buckle, and others suggest adjustable nylon collars. Rolled leather collars are also fine. Wide, flat leather collars are adequate but may wear away the hair around the neck. In addition, some leather collars stain the coat when wet.

Training collars. Training collars are also referred to as *choke collars*. This piece of equipment is essential for training dogs and solving behavior problems by allowing a mild correction to be administered with a tug on the leash. A metal training collar is recommended for a four-and-a-half-month-old Shepherd puppy only if he is particularly stubborn and difficult to manage. However, do not use a metal training collar on a sensitive dog until he is at least six months old.

A training collar is a rope of polished chain with a large metal ring at each end. Small rounded links are preferable. Nylon training collars are also very useful. Metal collars are preferred because of their smooth, quick release after being tightened around the dog's neck. Training collars are also available in rolled leather but do not operate as smoothly as those made of metal links. See Chapter Eight, "Obedience-Training Your German Shepherd," for more information.

Size is an important consideration. Measure the circumference of your dog's neck by wrapping a tape measure around it. Add three or four inches to the measured width and buy the correct size. Training collars come in even sizes.

A word of caution: Never leave an unsupervised puppy or grown dog with a training collar around his neck, not even if he is in a wire crate. Doing so can be a safety hazard.

Leashes

A puppy's first leash. To develop a loving, well-behaved dog, you must be able to control him, which involves attaching a leash to his collar. All puppies must be introduced to the idea of wearing a leash as well as having their movements controlled by the person holding the leash. Some dogs have an easier time with this concept than others. Before attempting to use a leash on a puppy, dog trainers recommend an adjustment process called "leash breaking." See Leash Breaking in Chapter Eight, "Obedience-Training Your German Shepherd" (page 116).

The all-purpose leash for grown dogs. Most dog trainers and breeders recommend a quality latigo leather leash three-fourths inch wide and six feet long with a brass-bolt snap for German Shepherds. This is the ideal leash for everyday use as well as for obedience training.

Some breeders prefer leashes made of nylon or cotton webbing for puppies and grown dogs. Leashes made of plastic or metal chain are not recommended. There is a consensus among experienced dog people that a six-foot leather leash is the safest, most durable type for training and everyday use. Leather softens with age, making it easier on the human hand. It also lasts longer than most other materials.

A leather leash beginning to wear develops thin sections, making it obvious that it needs to be replaced. This is important. If a weakened leash breaks when you are outdoors, your dog may bolt from you into traffic. Strength and comfort are the main considerations when selecting the proper leash for your dog.

Toys

Toys are thought of as objects designed for fun and entertainment. Toys for dogs, however, can be more. The right toys can prevent boredom and anxiety, which often lead to destructive behavior. Some toys help establish and reinforce the human-animal bond. Toys can also alleviate mild physical discomforts, such as teething, as well as promote development of the dog's mind and body.

Puppyhood and canine adolescence entail the development of the physical and mental ability to survive. Nature provides a learning process for this that includes various aspects of play behavior. A puppy or young dog's play promotes physical development, use of excess energy, establishment of territory or social rank, food-hunting skills, and maneuvers for getting out of threatening situations. German Shepherds' play usually has something to do with their instinct to guard, protect, or hunt. All these elements can be seen by observing a litter of Shepherd puppies piling into a heap, wrestling, pawing each other, and carrying objects around in their mouths as they roll and tumble with amusing exuberance.

Toys for your new dog should promote exercise, relieve boredom, alleviate the discomfort of teething, or provide an outlet for various

When a puppy plays ball, he is actually learning to chase and capture something. It's also a great way for Shepherds to use up some energy.

urges and desires. The best toys appeal to a dog's basic instincts. When playing, dogs learn to develop the skills that are necessary to survive in the wild, as though they were wolves. A puppy playing ball is actually learning to chase and capture something.

Plastic flying disks (Frisbees), when tossed, are wonderful for establishing a bond between a dog and members of his family as well as for satisfying many of the dog's instinctive urges. Tossing a disk or ball high into the air, though, is not recommended for puppies because of their soft joints, which may become injured as a result of jumping too high.

Because many dogs love stuffed toys, furry dog toys that squeak are highly recommended. They have no glass eyes or noses to swallow and do no damage when tossed around. Also recommended are the rubbery hive-shaped toys that bounce and roll in unexpected directions when tossed, as well as the latest generation of large, hard balls made of cressite rubber. These toys are not recommended for indoor use because of the physical action involved. Tennis balls are not suitable toys because they are small enough to swallow whole and lodge in the throat, causing a life-threatening situation. They can also be chewed into dangerous chunks that can be swallowed, possibly causing a serious blockage requiring surgery.

Teething is an irritating and sometimes painful stage for all puppies and young dogs. Appropriate chew toys can help satisfy the urge to chew without harming your dog or your family's possessions. Although rawhide chew toys (usually shaped like bones) are acceptable, bone-shaped toys made of hard nylon material are superior because they require more effort to gnaw down and make little or no demand on the digestive system. When properly used, they can be an effective aid in solving destructive chewing problems.

For dog toys to be safe, they must be well constructed and not easily destroyed. Dog owners can prevent medical problems by discarding old or half-chewed toys before pieces can be swallowed. No toy should be small enough to swallow. Avoid toys containing toxic materials, such as lead-based paint. Do not buy items with small parts that can be chewed off and swallowed, such as metal bells or rivets. Remove strings and ribbons.

If you purchase a chew toy that simulates something real in your home, such as a shoe or a book, you run the risk of teaching your dog to chew the real thing. Pet owners should reject all manner of pulling games. Games and toys that involve any version of tug-of-war stimulate the aggressive aspects of dog behavior and can lead to nipping, growling, and biting.

Grooming Tools

Brushes. The first part of a grooming session involves brushing the coat. Brushing loosens and removes dead hair; it also stimulates the hair follicles and promotes the secretion of natural oils that soften the skin and coat the hairs. Every puppy or adult dog needs one or more brush types. A natural bristle brush and a slicker brush are the types most used for optimum coat care of this breed. Consult a professional groomer or pet supplies dealer regarding the type and size best suited for your dog.

A *natural bristle brush* is the most standard of all dog brushes and is useful for almost every type of coat. Bristle brushes come in a variety of sizes and shapes, including soft, medium, and hard bristles. Selection should be based on the age of your dog and the length and texture of his coat. Use common sense when making a selection. The bristles should be tapered, with some that are long enough to penetrate down to the dog's skin. Natural bristles are superior to synthetic bristles because their tips are not sharp and harsh. Consequently, they are less abrasive on the skin and hair coat. Natural bristle brushes also last longer, in part because they are set in a durable base, such as hardwood or foam rubber over thick quality plastic. The flexibility of soft natural bristles reduces friction and discomfort for the dog and helps avoid static electricity, which twists and tangles the hair.

The *slicker brush* is an odd-looking rectangular tool, with a long handle and short, bent-wire teeth usually set in foam rubber. The metal teeth are like no others seen on a brush. This highly useful tool can be obtained in small, medium, and large sizes. Grooming a German Shepherd requires a slicker brush when the dog is shedding heavily. If used too frequently or too vigorously, it may split the hair ends and cause *brush burn* (inflammation of the skin). The slicker brush is used to remove dead hair from the German Shepherd coat and to untangle clumps or tufts of fur.

Combs. Combing a dog's coat usually follows a thorough brushing. The purpose of combing is to smooth out the coat and further stimulate the hair follicles. It also helps prevent the coat from matting and twisting. Combing a dog's coat makes him look good.

Medium-spaced comb. All German Shepherd owners should have this basic grooming tool for daily or twice-weekly use. The thick, medium-length German Shepherd coat requires a comb with medium-spaced teeth that are 1 to 1½ inches long. Ideally, your comb should have twelve teeth to the inch in order to untangle clumped or matted hair. Medium-spaced combs should be made of smooth metal and are available with Teflon-coated tips to add ease and smoothness to combing out a dog. Stainless-steel combs are considered to be the best made.

Flea comb. Although a flea comb does exactly what its name implies, removing fleas is not its only use. It is also useful for combing out the softer, finer hairs, especially in the Shepherd's undercoat. Flea combs have very fine teeth spaced close together. Some are made with handles, and some are not.

Shedding blade. This handy and easy-to-use tool strips away dead hair quickly and conveniently. It is especially good for breeds that are seasonal or constant shedders, such as the German Shepherd. It is a thin metal blade that has been bent around to form a large, tear-shaped loop and is held together with a leather handle. It resembles a severely bent hacksaw blade with serrated teeth on its cutting edge.

Undercoat rake. English or German rakes are yet another tool useful for ridding the coat of dead hair, especially on the softer undercoat of the German Shepherd Dog. A rake is recommended by many Shepherd breeders and looks like a metal comb attached to a wooden handle—resembling a miniature garden rake. The metal teeth may be spaced apart in various widths. Some rakes are made with long coarse teeth that are interspersed with shorter fine teeth for the efficient removal of shedding hair.

Other grooming tools and supplies that are necessary for German Shepherd Dogs are a guillotine-type nail trimmer; a canine toothbrush; various types of dog shampoo (tearless, flea, etc.); coat conditioners (highly recommended); distilled water in a spray bottle or anti-static coat spray for brushing; a hose-type spray (for baths); a blow dryer (for after baths); a commercial ear cleaner; cotton balls; a grooming table (optional); powdered coagulant (to stop nails from bleeding when clipped too close to the quick).

Coming home with a new puppy is like bringing a newborn baby into the house. Like any new mother and father, you must provide the youngster with everything he will need—from food to love to learning how to behave. It is the normal order of things.

If you treat your puppy as a new baby and take care of his needs, you will be rewarded with a happy, healthy dog. All the gear discussed in this chapter will help ease the transition for everyone, but especially for the newest member of your family. If your new dog has not yet arrived, buy the things the dog needs before he comes home for the first time. If the dog is already enjoying your hospitality, go out and get the items recommended here. It is never too late. It all goes to make the first day and all the days that follow as wonderful as possible.

◆ ◆ ◆

CHAPTER SIX

Feeding Your Dog

Feeding a dog, from puppyhood to old age, is of enormous importance and is one of the areas in which dog owners can significantly influence their pets' health and well-being. Because of continuing advances in nutritional science, the pet food industry has been able to make it easy for everyone to properly feed their dogs. Through extensive research, pet food manufacturers have learned how to formulate dog foods so that they provide the required nutrients in correct proportions for growth, day-to-day maintenance, pregnancy, lactation, hard work, and various stressful conditions, such as cold weather or extreme emotions.

When prey animals are plentiful, wolves (or dogs) living in the wild get a complete and balanced diet by eating what they hunt, which is usually grass-eating herbivores. The first part of a kill that is eaten is the viscera and the stomach contents, which, along with the bones and muscle meat, provide carbohydrates, vitamins, minerals, and fiber—all needed to create a complete and balanced diet. Companion animals living in our homes must also obtain the same high level of nourishment as their cousins in the wild if they are to live long and healthy lives. In order to achieve this goal, dog owners must feed their pets a proper diet. Feeding a dog a complete and balanced diet makes life easier for the family and healthier for the dog.

In the wild, wolves (or dogs) must search for their food to survive. They hunt in packs and eat the prey animals they are able to capture. With that accomplished, they consume as much as they possibly can in one meal because they cannot be sure when they will eat again.

This seemingly gluttonous behavior is the source of the expression "wolfing down your food."

It is a fact that German Shepherds love to eat as much as they love to do anything, perhaps more. However, if you compare the behavioral and medical difficulties of finicky dogs that refuse to eat, overeating is easier to cope with. Still, a German Shepherd can eat itself into unattractive obesity, serious health problems, and a shortened life span if its family allows it to happen. The problem is not what the dog eats. The problem is what the dog is fed. It is the pet owner's obligation to control the quality and quantity of a dog's diet.

Food for Thought

Most breeders and professional dog people recommend high-quality, brand-name commercial dog foods for German Shepherds. These foods contain quality ingredients with all the essential nutritional requirements for dogs in addition to being highly digestible and palatable. Commercial dog foods are made in several forms and vary in their moisture content, shape, density, texture, and ingredients. Convenience, palatability, cost, and the quality of the food are the deciding factors when selecting one commercial product from another.

Some people prefer to feed their dogs preparations made in their own kitchens. To do this properly requires a knowledge of the minimum daily requirements of dogs and the precise nutritional ratios of protein, carbohydrates, fat, vitamins, and minerals. When these nutritional essentials are ignored or unknown, a wide assortment of health problems may result. At their best, homemade meals for dogs must be carefully formulated and fed with regard to the dog's minimum daily requirements. At their worst, home-cooked meals consist of table scraps and leftovers, haphazardly fed to the dog for the sake of convenience, cost, and avoidance of waste. No breeder, handler, veterinarian, or other professional dog person advocates this approach to feeding dogs.

Superior commercial dog food is available in supermarkets, pet food shops, and feed stores or from veterinarians. It can be obtained in three forms: dry food, canned food, and semimoist food.

Dry dog food. These grain or cereal types are packaged as meals, pellets, biscuits, kibbles (broken biscuits), or expanded products. The hard-baked biscuits are usually shaped like bones.

High-quality dry dog food contains approximately 1,500 calories per pound. It is 10 percent moisture. Beef, chicken, or lamb mixed with cereal grains are the primary ingredients of dry dog foods, which may also contain soybean products, milk products, vitamin and mineral supplements, various animal protein sources, and fats and oils (sprayed on the surface for palatability). Most dogs are attracted to high-quality dry dog food. However, it is more appealing when the food is substantially moistened. Dogs will eat approximately 20 percent more when water or other liquid has been added.

Dry food costs less money than other types of food, is more convenient, and does not spoil as quickly as canned food. Manufacturers of brand-name dry dog food claim that their products do not require vitamin and mineral supplements. Most veterinarians agree. Dry dog food has become the most popular dog food used.

Canned dog food. The main feature of canned dog food is its very high moisture content—on average, between 74 percent and 78 percent.

Canned dog foods are produced in two general forms: 1. the canned meat type, which contains mostly meat and poultry along with their by-products, fat, a small quantity of soy products, plus added vitamins and minerals, and 2. mixed or standard canned ration, which contains large quantities of cereal grains, soybean products, fat, meat and meat by-products, plus vitamin and mineral supplements.

Canned foods are appealing to dogs because of their abundant water and fat content, which affects smell, taste, and appearance. They contain between 500 and 600 calories per 14- to 15-ounce can, depending on the brand, the size, and the contents. Experienced Shepherd people use canned foods as a flavoring to dry food in lesser amounts or restrict them to a transitional diet for puppies being weaned from mother's milk to solid food. Feeding a German Shepherd canned food exclusively is not recommended. It's impractical and very expensive.

Semimoist food. Semimoist food has the appearance of ground or cubed meat in color, texture, and shape. It contains 25 percent to 30 percent moisture and provides between 1,350 and 1,500 calories per pound. This food type contains animal products (meat and meat by-products), milk products, fats and oils, soybean products, and mineral and vitamin supplements. Semimoist dog food is complete and balanced and may be fed as the primary diet.

Some dog owners use semimoist food as a supplement to other types of food, including homemade meals. It is odorless to humans but attractive and highly palatable to dogs. This type of dog food requires no refrigeration and comes in premeasured portions. It has a high sugar content and costs considerably more than dry food. Feeding your Shepherd a diet consisting of semimoist food exclusively during housebreaking training is undesirable, as it tends to increase the dog's water intake, which in turn increases the dog's frequency of urination.

Dog biscuits and snacks. Manufactured dog biscuits are another form of dry dog food. They have high nutritional value and can be used as part of a dog's daily diet. Check the label to be sure that the biscuits are consistent with the ingredients of high-quality dog food. Hard-baked biscuits (usually shaped like bones) as well as other type of snacks have become quite popular as rewards for good behavior and expressions of affection.

Snack products are used to supplement the dog's usual diet and are given as an expression of love and approval. Some pet owners use commercial snack foods as part of their dogs' diet, but most veterinarians believe this is not essential.

When used sparingly as treats, these food products serve to strengthen and promote the bond between dogs and their families. They are also used by some dog trainers as a reward for good performance.

The ingredients of these foods vary widely in their nutritional value. Generally speaking, they are often higher in salt, fat, and sugar content and are not recommended as a total dog ration. Snacks should not represent more than 10 percent of your dog's daily food intake.

Feeding a Balanced Diet

When selecting a commercial dog food for your German Shepherd, choose one that is labeled "complete and balanced" or words to that effect. Dog foods on the shelves of supermarkets and pet food shops may or may not offer this important advantage. Such labeling indicates that the ingredients of the product are not only of high quality but are combined in the proper proportions and contain the necessary nutrients to satisfy a dog's established energy requirements.

A number of variables determine how much to feed a dog and, to some degree, what to feed (more or less protein or fat, for example). The nutritional requirements of dogs vary, depending on age, metabolism, activity level, and lifestyle.

Adult dogs living as pets do not require as much food as dogs in other stages of life or in exceptional situations. The intensive-growth period of puppies, for example (eight weeks to twelve months), creates the need for them to consume more food than at any other time in their lives. Consequently, growing puppies require more calories per pound of body weight than adult dogs. Pregnant females or those nursing a litter of puppies require more food because of the greater demands made on their bodies. Hard-working, active dogs, such as field dogs or protection dogs, cannot survive without the added energy from greater quantities of food with increased fat content, especially if they are outdoors in cold weather. Dogs that are physically or emotionally stressed also need to be fed more food than usual to maintain their health. *Do not rely on general statements when deciding about your Shepherd's diet. Ask you dog's breeder, veterinarian, or professional trainer to help you determine what to feed your dog and in what specific amount.*

Feeding Guidelines for German Shepherd Dogs

Most breeders and experienced Shepherd owners feed their dogs a high-quality, dry dog food with a high fat and protein content. How much to feed a dog depends on many factors, as noted above. A healthy dog's appetite is based on his energy requirements.

Puppies become fully grown dogs slightly before or slightly after the second birthday. The quantity of food eaten diminishes dramatically as they approach adulthood. Young dogs tell you when to reduce the quantity of food by leaving much of it in the bowl. If a puppy eats all the food in his bowl for three days in a row, increase the amount slightly. If food is left in the bowl for three days in a row, decrease the amount slightly.

A healthy German Shepherd puppy getting proper nutrition maintains a steady rate of growth; a full, glossy coat; and a slight thickness of fat beneath the skin.

As an adult, your Shepherd requires a consistent diet that offers no more or less than his lifestyle requires. Although he requires fewer calories per pound than he did as a puppy, he may require more food than he did as a puppy simply because he weighs more.

Establish your dog's ideal or desired body weight (with the help of a breeder or a veterinarian). Feed him a high-quality ration that will maintain the established body weight. Initially, weigh your dog once a week to determine whether the food is adding or subtracting body weight. If his weight fluctuates up or down by more than 10 percent from the established ideal weight, adjust the ration by feeding him more or less food.

The nutritional requirements of two dogs of the same age and weight, even from the same litter of puppies, may vary as much as 100 percent; one dog may require twice as much food as the other. Once you determine how much to feed, check the dog's weight once a month to be sure you are able to maintain his ideal weight. Always measure the amount of food you give your dog. Do not estimate the amount.

How to weigh your dog. First, weigh yourself on a bathroom scale. Second, hold the dog in your arms and weigh yourself again. Subtract the first figure from the second figure to determine your dog's exact weight.

Amounts of food. It is difficult to make a general statement about exact amounts of food because of the differences in nutritional requirements from one dog to another. When deciding how much to feed your adult dog, use this handy shortcut: one pound of premium dry food feeds approximately sixty pounds of dog per day.

One can of high-quality dog food feeds approximately twenty pounds of dog per day (based on 500 calories per twenty pounds). A sixty-pound dog, therefore, requires approximately three cans per day.

One patty of semimoist food is approximately equal to one-half can of dog food. Thus, one patty feeds approximately ten pounds of dog per day. A sixty-pound dog requires six semimoist patties per day.

These generalized amounts are merely guidelines for average dogs living average lives. Each dog must be evaluated on an individual basis, taking into consideration the differences in metabolic rate, size, temperament, environment, and work routine, if any. Consult a veterinarian for more specific instructions concerning your own dog.

Feeding Premium Dry Food

(The following amounts are for the typical house dog's maintenance and not for working, pregnant, or performance dogs.)

Puppies (weaned to eight weeks): Feed three-fourths cup dry food *four times a day.*

Puppies (eight weeks to six months): Feed one cup dry food *three times a day* (depending on age, size, and activity level). Some three-month-old puppies or older puppies may refuse their midday meal. Add the food to the morning and evening meals. If the young dog leaves food in the bowl, eliminate one cup (more or less) from the daily ration.

Adults (one year and older): Feed two and a half cups dry food *twice a day.*

It is important to soak dry food in the bowl.

Pour water in the bowl, enough to barely cover the food, and let it sit for fifteen minutes before feeding it to the dog. The food will absorb most of the liquid and resemble a meat-type ration.

It is important to soak dry food because German Shepherds, like most large, deep-chested dogs, are vulnerable to a life-threatening medical condition commonly known as bloat. See Gastric Dilation-Volvulus in Chapter Twelve, "Medical Problems Common to the German Shepherd Dog" (page 194).

Veterinarians and breeders recommend soaking dry food in a liquid for fifteen minutes before feeding it to the dog. The liquid expands the food in the bowl rather than in the dog's stomach and slows down the rate of food consumption. Soaking the food may also alter a dog's ravenous eating behavior. It could possibly reduce the creation of intestinal gas, thereby possibly reducing the risk of bloat. It is a theory.

Most experienced owners and breeders feed their Shepherds a premium, high-quality dry dog food with a high fat content. Among this group, many mix the dry ration with canned food.

Premium dog foods formulated for "puppies" or "growth stage" are used by some breeders but not by others, who believe that puppy foods accelerate weight gain and the rate of growth and that, along with improper exercise, they can create orthopedic problems.

Although supplemental foods and snacks are not necessary, they are as pleasing for the owner to give as they are for the dog to receive. Supplemental foods, however, should be healthful and nutritious. We recommend that you occasionally indulge your German Shepherd with a special health treat of small quantities of cottage cheese, plain yogurt, scrambled eggs, fruits and vegetables (cooked or raw) such as grapes, apples, green beans, or carrots. Among the most-often used food treats that Shepherds love are dog biscuits, which can be offered as a reward or gesture of approval. Added foods may be given before, after, during, or between meals but in small portions.

All breeders agree that Shepherds are easy to feed. They'll eat everything and beg for more if you permit it. Do not overfeed them, especially puppies. There is a consensus among German Shepherd people that a breed prone to hip dysplasia, such as this one, must not become too big too soon. (See Hip Dysplasia in Chapter Twelve, "Medical Problems Common to the German Shepherd Dog," page 196.)

Do not feed your dog chocolate of any kind (it is toxic to dogs), raw eggs (they are difficult to digest, and raw egg white is especially harmful), or raw meat or fish (they may be contaminated by dangerous internal parasites).

Some Shepherds become obsessed with food, especially as they get older. Dog owners should know that it's okay if their pets are a bit leaner than those in the show ring.

Overweight Dogs

To determine whether your dog is overweight, feel around his chest. Run your palm along the ribs on each side. A healthy, normal dog should not retain very much fat between the skin and the ribs. A dog of normal weight will have a thin layer of fat covering the rib cage, enough for a slight finger indentation when pressed. One-fifth inch of tissue covering the ribs is the appropriate thickness. If the shape of the ribs cannot be seen, the dog is probably obese. Fat protrusions are obvious, particularly under the stomach or chin or on torsos that resemble a rounded, shapeless cylinder from neck to tail. These are the definite indications of obesity. Excluding medical conditions and inherited traits, overweight is almost always the result of consuming more calories (from too much food) than are needed to grow, reproduce, or function.

Because the majority of German Shepherds do most of their growing within the first twelve to twenty-four months of life, they require more food during this period than at any other time in their lives. This is often misinterpreted by pet owners as the animal's normal food intake. When the dog suddenly stops eating large amounts, the owner believes the dog is sick and rewards him with love and affection for eating more than he wants. Unfortunately, these good intentions harm the family pet's health by creating an association of food with love and approval. Food should be nothing more or less than the source of life-sustaining nutrition.

CHAPTER SEVEN

Housebreaking Your German Shepherd Dog

All dogs can and should be housebroken, including the German Shepherd Dog. Fortunately, this breed accepts housebreaking quite easily and has no problems with the techniques. Only those with medical problems have any difficulties, and even they can be housebroken when the medical problem is corrected. A puppy of eight weeks or older can begin this program and be housebroken within one week. Depending upon the dog, the owners, and consistent adherence to the program, the average German Shepherd Dog can be housebroken in three days to three weeks. Puppies and young dogs still require confinement after they have been housebroken until they're proven reliable, which could take as long as two years.

Housebreaking means your dog is trained to urinate and defecate *outdoors* on a schedule of your choosing based on your needs. The dog must *always* relieve himself in a convenient location outdoors. He must *always* control himself until he can be taken out. The dog is never allowed to relieve himself indoors.

Housebreaking is not paper training and has nothing to do with the use of newspapers on the floor. Housebreaking is the only sensible option because it is not practical to paper-train German Shepherds. They are large dogs that eliminate in great quantities. Paper training and housebreaking involve methods that are similar in some aspects but quite different in others. These two methods of training have conflicting objectives. Housebreaking is the only technique recommended for German Shepherd Dogs.

Many novice dog owners use newspapers on the floor as a temporary measure until their puppy is able to go outside. Some puppies and adult dogs are encouraged to eliminate on newspapers, indoors as well as on the ground. Doing both prolongs housebreaking with only marginal success. Utilizing both methods tends to confuse the dog, causing "accidents" and "mistakes."

Eliminating over newspapers teaches a dog to relieve himself on your floor and to claim (and constantly reclaim) territory in your home by marking it with the scent of his urine and feces. This is called *scent marking.* Some dogs mark their scent with their urine in many places in your home. It is difficult for them to confine this instinctive behavior to one spot on the floor after they have been encouraged to use newspapers. Paper training teaches dogs to use the floor.

The best situation is to begin housebreaking your puppy the minute he comes to live with you, ideally at eight weeks of age. This may conflict with instructions from your veterinarian, who advises you to keep your young dog indoors until he gets all his vaccinations; this may not be accomplished until the puppy is four months old. We do not suggest that you ignore your veterinarian's advice. However, you must understand that allowing your puppy to relieve himself on newspapers before getting him to go outdoors, without soiling in your house, causes behavioral confusion. The changeover will take longer and demand greater effort and patience on your part.

Procedures and Technique for Housebreaking

The elements of this housebreaking program are 1. the feed-water-walk schedule, 2. feeding your dog during housebreaking, 3. removing odors of past mistakes, 4. confinement, and 5. correction and praise. These elements will work only when used together. To leave out any one of them during the housebreaking process will ensure failure. All aspects of the five-part program are valid for the life of the dog, with the exception of confinement. Confinement is necessary until the dog is proven reliable.

1. The Feed-Water-Walk Schedule

Dogs living indoors benefit most from a schedule regulating their food, water, and elimination. The object is to condition the dog's mind and body to eliminating body waste at specific times of the day and night. Daily repetition of feeding, drinking, and walking at the same times creates in the dog's mind and body a timing mechanism that will last a lifetime. Depending upon the size of the dog, his age, the amount he eats, and his house training, it will take three to six hours after feeding for the food to travel through his digestive system and leave his body. Obviously, puppies digest food much sooner than grown dogs. By learning your dog's digestion time, you can predict when he must relieve himself. The schedule must be adjusted to suit other physical needs as well. For example, puppies, with smaller bladders and stomachs and immature sphincter muscles, must be walked more frequently than mature dogs. Because eating and drinking stimulate elimination (peristalsis), most dogs relieve themselves immediately after eating. Consult your veterinarian for your dog's digestion time.

By always feeding, watering, and walking your dog at the same times every day, you teach him to create a body clock with an inner schedule consistent with your schedule. This inner schedule will continue after the housebreaking program is finished. The dog becomes motivated to control his need to eliminate because his body clock anticipates walks at specific times every day.

Bear in mind that a dog's age determines the type of schedule you create for him. A young dog must be fed more often than a fully grown dog. During the major growth period (three to twelve months of age), puppies require more food per pound of body weight than older dogs do. They should not eat their entire daily ration at one meal. They need to eliminate more frequently, and that means more walks. Young puppies should be walked according to the schedule below.

Mature dogs do not need as many walks (for the purpose of elimination) as younger, smaller dogs. They can control their need to relieve themselves for much longer periods of time.

When you are setting up a feed-water-walk schedule, the first walk of the day should be determined by how many hours have passed since the dog was last walked. *There must not be a nighttime interval longer than eight hours.* If your dog's last walk was at 11:00 P.M., his first walk the next morning should be at 7:00 A.M. Here are some suggested schedules that can be used exactly as they are or adjusted to take into account the needs of your dog or your family.

Schedule for Puppies Two to Six Months Old

7:00 A.M.	Walk the dog.
7:30 A.M.	Feed, water, and walk.
11:30 A.M.	Feed, water, and walk.
4:30 P.M.	Feed, water, and walk.
8:30 P.M.	Water and walk (last water of the day).
11:00 P.M.	Walk the dog.

Schedule for Dogs Six Months to One Year Old

7:00 A.M.	Walk the dog.
7:30 A.M.	Feed, water, and walk.
12:30 P.M.	Water and walk.
4:30 P.M.	Feed, water, and walk.
7:30 P.M.	Water and walk (last water of the day).
11:00 P.M.	Walk the dog.

Schedule for Dogs One Year and Older

7:00 A.M.	Walk the dog.
7:30 A.M.	Feed, water, and walk.
4:30 P.M.	Water and walk.
7:30 P.M.	Water and walk (last water of the day).
11:00 P.M.	Walk the dog.

Schedule for Dogs of Those Who Go to Work

First thing in the morning — Walk the dog.

Before leaving for work — Feed, water, and walk.

Midday — Have a neighbor or hired walker feed, water, and walk a puppy (only water and walk a grown dog).

Home from work — Walk the dog.

Immediately after walk — Feed, water, and walk a puppy or dog less than one year old (only water and walk a grown dog).

Early evening — Water and walk (last water of the day).

Before going to bed — Walk the dog.

When walking your new dog or puppy for the first time, bear in mind your pet's need to mark or scent his own territory with his urine. This instinct works to your advantage. Allow your dog to seek out the scent marks of other dogs and eliminate over them. These will become permanent stations along the path of your dog's daily walks. Congratulate and praise your dog every time he relieves himself anyplace outdoors. An important part of the teaching process is to praise him for doing the right thing and correct him when he does the wrong thing.

2. Feeding Your Dog During Housebreaking

Meeting your dog's nutritional requirements should always be the first consideration when selecting a proper diet. However, during the housebreaking period there is another equally important goal. It is essential that the dog's digestion be in perfect order or the housebreaking program will fail. If your dog develops loose stools, diarrhea, or the need to urinate excessively, it will be impossible for him to follow any of the feed-water-walk schedules and he will not become trained.

Feed your dog his normal ration as recommended in Chapter Six, "Feeding Your Dog." Moistened dry dog food is highly recommended to maintain a firm stool and allow for successful housebreaking. Do not overfeed your dog. However, puppies must be allowed to eat as much as they want for growth. If your dog leaves food in the bowl or is defecating excessively, you are feeding him too much. Reduce his food portion according to what is left uneaten in the bowl. Do not feed your dog between-meal snacks or leftovers from the table. Adhere to the feeding schedule with great consistency.

Your dog's stomach is sensitive. Any sudden changes in his diet will cause diarrhea, and that will bring the housebreaking process to a halt. If you are going to change your dog's diet, do not make the switch suddenly. Hold off on housebreaking until the change is completed. Over a four-day period, add one-fourth new food to three-fourths of the old food, increasing the amount by fourths each time as you decrease the old food by the same amount. Once you have settled all the questions about your dog's diet, you may begin the housebreaking program.

3. Removing Odors of Past Mistakes

A dog's scenting ability is the greatest of all his senses. Picture the human nose and then compare it to the canine muzzle. Inside each is a fine lining that is a membrane containing thousands of smell receptors (in humans) and millions of receptors (in dogs). In humans this area is less than one inch long. In dogs it can be four inches long. Smells trigger electric impulses to the olfactory center in the brain, arriving there as raw information to be evaluated. Dogs use their noses more than their eyes and maintain a memory storage in the brain based on smells. The canine sense of smell is extraordinary.

It is impossible to housebreak a dog unless you obliterate all past odors of his own urine and defecation. This includes past mistakes on the carpet and areas of the floor where he was permitted to use newspapers as a toilet. Every time the dog relieves himself on the floor, an odor remains, no matter how well you may scrub it away. This remaining odor draws the dog back to that spot and triggers his instinct to "mark" on top of it. It is a continuing cycle that can be ended only when the dog's scent of urine or feces is eliminated. This explains why dogs with housebreaking problems always seem to relieve themselves in the same locations. Although the odor may not be evident to the human nose, it is perceptible to the intricate smell mechanism of a dog's nose. Buy an odor neutralizer concentrate at a pet supply store or mail-order catalog and use it according to the instructions. This type of product is the only means available to obliterate previous scent marks in your house successfully. Ammonia, bleach, vinegar, and other household products do not mask the odors of body waste from the dog's keen sense of smell. Odor neutralizers do not remove or perfume the smells; they alter them. (It is important to note that ammonia intensifies the odor of urine and tends to attract animals rather than repel them.)

4. Confinement

Puppies that are not housebroken will relieve themselves about every hour (depending on their activity level and water intake) and will do it on the floor, in front of you. Adolescent and mature dogs who have experienced your displeasure have greater sphincter control and will wait until you leave before letting go on the carpet. It is not defiance, arrogance, spite, or stupidity that makes them behave this way. They are simply unhousebroken dogs caught in the crossfire between human demands and their natural inclinations. Their bodies have not been regulated and they have not been taught (in a manner they can understand) what you expect of them.

Restricting your dog's indoor movements (especially when no one is home) is a key factor for a successful housebreaking program. During the housebreaking program, confine your dog or puppy if you do not have time to watch for the signs that tell you he is going to relieve himself. (Dogs and puppies sniff close to the ground, whimper and whine, make gagging sounds, turn in circles, and even head for the door when they must eliminate.) If you are going to leave the house, it is essential that the dog in the housebreaking program be confined to one small area of your home until you return.

Dogs are born with the instinct not to soil their eating and sleep-

ing area. They are also taught this by their mothers. When you confine your dog, he quickly realizes that he will be forced to remain in
the same area with his urine and feces if he lets go. Sometimes a dog
cannot help himself and soils his own area anyway. However, he has
not soiled the entire house, creating more aggravation (and scent areas to return to).

Do not mistake "confinement" for imprisonment or tying the dog
down someplace. Simply confine the dog in a small but comfortable
area adequate for his physical and psychological needs. Leave him in
the selected confinement area with his food, water, toys, and bedding. A puppy gate installed in the doorway will keep him there.
Double gates (one placed on top of the other) are necessary for
grown dogs so that they cannot jump over.

The kitchen is the most commonly chosen confinement site because of the size, location, and floor covering. Linoleum or floor tiles
will withstand your dog's "accidents" better than any other covering.
This is the ideal place. You may also use a bathroom or small hallway
for this purpose. The area should be large enough for the dog to walk
around without feeling punished, and he should be able to see other
parts of the house and family activities.

Never confine your dog or puppy behind a closed door. This is
psychologically harmful and counterproductive. Some owners have
successfully housebroken their dogs using the same wire dog crates
purchased for other confinement purposes. Many breeders recommend them, although they are not necessary for housebreaking unless you have no other practical area for confinement. Choose a wire
dog crate that is the correct size for your dog, with enough room for
him to stand up and turn around in. It can serve as a confinement
area, provided that the dog is not left in it for an entire day.

During the housebreaking program, confine your dog when you
leave the house or do not have time to watch for his mistakes. *Do not
lay any newspapers down on the floor in the confinement area.* If the dog has
an accident on the floor, take him outside and praise him lavishly if
he eliminates there. Clean up the mess from the floor, get rid of the
scent with an odor neutralizer, and continue the program as outlined.

Using newspapers on the floor only teaches the dog to use the floor and prevents the successful conclusion to housebreaking.

It is good for the dog to run around loose as much as possible. Release him from confinement when you get home. The dog should be allowed to run around in the house, provided that someone watches him for signs that he has to relieve himself.

5. Correction and Praise

This is the fifth element of housebreaking, the most important part of the program. If your dog relieves himself inside the house in front of you, rattle a shake can vigorously and say, "NO," in a loud, firm voice to impress him with your displeasure. To make a shake can, take an empty soda can, wash it, and insert ten pennies into it. Tape the opening so the pennies cannot fall out. Shake the can vigorously. It will make a very loud, commanding rattle similar to the sound of a New Year's Eve noisemaker. It is an effective way to correct a dog, especially a puppy. It easily gets his attention when shaken loudly. It enables you to deliver a correction from across the room without the use of a leash. However, the manner in which you say, "NO," should be based on your dog's sensitivity. A puppy or overly sensitive dog cannot tolerate an overbearing manner or even a shake can too vigorously rattled. You do not want to terrorize your dog. You simply want to get his attention and deliver a corrective reprimand.

Your dog will probably stop eliminating if your correction was firm enough (for his personality). Place a leash and choke collar on him and quickly take him outside to the place where he is supposed to relieve himself. Praise him the minute you get there, whether he relieves himself or not. If he continues to eliminate in the correct area, lavish him with tremendous praise. This praise and correction is an important element of the teaching process. Place several shake cans around the house for warnings and keep the dog's leash and choke collar handy. If you cannot reach a shake can in time, say, "NO," in a loud, firm tone of voice and then take the dog out. Praise him afterward.

The only language that communicates between dogs and humans is the one of positive and negative messages. It is precisely how dogs communicate between themselves. Dogs thrive on acceptance and praise. When these are denied and negative messages are substituted, most dogs correct their behavior. It is the only known teaching process available for domestic dogs.

The most common misconception that dog owners have is the meaning of the term "correction." It is often confused with the word "punishment." Punishment is a penalizing act for wrongdoing that involves harsh or painful treatment. In dog training, a correction is different. A correction is nothing more than a negative message to a dog that he was incorrect or did not behave properly. Corrections must be humane and nonabusive in order to preserve the pleasant relationship between dog and human as well as to teach in a positive way.

Punishing a dog for destructive behavior, for example, may offer a temporary emotional release, but it teaches a dog nothing except to fear you. *Punishment is not teaching.* If your dog misbehaves, your objective should be to solve the problem, not to punish the dog. These are two different matters.

Corrections, or negative messages, are simple, humane techniques for communicating to a dog that he has done the wrong thing. The *corrective jerk* is the most effective and most frequently used correction technique available to dog owners. It delivers a mild, negative sensation with the use of a leash and choke collar. It must not be performed in a manner that hurts the dog. The reason dogs interpret it as a negative message is that it is always accompanied with the verbal reprimand "NO." The jerk of the leash and the slight tightening of the choke collar (for an instant) are associated with the owner's criticism and lack of approval. The correction is part of the teaching process.

Praise is a reward. It motivates a dog to do whatever it is that you expect of him. You should always praise him for his efforts. If he misbehaves or fails to execute a command, correct him with the corrective jerk, the rattle of a shake can, or by saying, "NO," in a firm tone of voice. *After every correction it is essential that you immediately praise your dog.* It reassures him and rewards him for trying to do the right thing.

Do not correct your dog for messing in the house unless you catch him in the act. Your dog has no way of associating your correction with a house-soiling "accident" if it happened more than ten seconds before you discovered it. Correcting him later would be useless and unkind. Never yell, hit, swat with a newspaper, or rub your dog's nose in his own mess. It is unthinkable to hit a child for making a mistake when you are teaching him or her something new. The same is true for a dog. Do not slap a newspaper against your hand as a correction. It threatens the dog and is simply a form of punishment. Your hands should only be associated with good things, such as expressions of affection. The objective is not to frighten the dog but to tell him that he has just done something wrong. The next step is to teach him the correct thing to do.

CHAPTER EIGHT

Obedience-Training Your German Shepherd

German Shepherds are among the easiest breeds to teach. They are famous for their desire to please. Training a typical Shepherd puppy is fun for the dog and his family, and that attitude should be reflected every time you work with the dog. The essence of this dog-training course involves love, praise, and corrections.

Obedience training is based on a dog's acceptance of the human's higher-ranking position and the animal's need to have someone leading his pack. In the training course offered here, the dog is rewarded with praise each time he carries out a command properly. He is corrected when he does not obey the command or perform it properly (*only after it has been taught to him*). This establishes the trainer as the leader of the dog's pack.

The Training Course

The training elements of SIT, SIT-STAY, HEEL and Automatic SIT, DOWN, DOWN-STAY, and COME WHEN CALLED offered in this chapter encompass a complete basic obedience training course. We cover step-by-step details for teaching your dog each of the six basic commands. We also offer the proper use of praise and corrections as motivational techniques. These training elements will help you communicate with your dog on a meaningful level. Obedience training is the language of dogs and people and makes life better for everyone.

Training Sessions

Training puppies (seven weeks to six months). A very young puppy (up to three months old) should not wear a training collar with which to be corrected. Young puppies respond properly to gentle leash corrections with a regular collar. Use a leather or nylon collar with a buckle. Few, if any, puppies ever perform obedience commands with precision, no matter what type of collar they wear.

Do not overwork a young puppy. Restricting sessions to ten minutes several times a day will prevent him from becoming bored. If the dog does something right, praise him and move on to something else. If you do not have the dog's attention, it means you are not making it fun. You may be pushing the puppy too hard or too long. This will only produce a bored and resentful dog and will not have a positive effect on you, either. Although obedience training is not playtime, it should not be hard work. It is important to make sure the puppy or young dog responds on the first command by placing him in position with your hands, if necessary. Corrections should be gentle but firm, not harsh — and certainly not abusive.

Training adolescent dogs (six to eighteen months). Adolescents are capable of longer sessions and greater precision than puppies. Take into account your dog's stamina, attention span, and personality. No two dogs are alike. If your Shepherd is obedient but is looking away or has lost his enthusiasm, you have practiced too long. End your sessions with the successful completion of a command and before the dog loses interest.

After teaching each command, it is important to keep practicing it until the next session. By all means practice in the yard or in the house all the commands your dog has learned, letting him know that he must listen to you wherever he is and at all times. Throw commands such as "SIT-STAY" at the door, "SIT-STAY" for his food, and so on, into your everyday life.

Do not give commands to your dog while he is off-leash or in situations where you do not have control. This will encourage your puppy or young dog to disregard you and test your authority. The adolescent Shepherd is going to test you at some point, so early training requiring a consistent response is extremely important.

Training adult dogs (eighteen months and older). Training the adult dog can be as much fun as training a puppy but with quicker results. It must still be fun but consistent, with fair corrections. Some adult Shepherds have stubborn moments and can put their owners to the test. Do not train your dog if you are tired or in a bad mood. Skip it until you feel better. Shepherds are sensitive and respond negatively to inappropriate or harsh human behavior. On the other hand, the ideal tonic for changing your mood and cheering yourself up may be a training session with your dog (or puppy).

Praise

In this training course rewarding your dog for obeying and performing properly comes in the form of verbal praise, usually as enthusiastic compliments such as, "Good boy. What a good dog!" At times an affectionate pat on the body makes an appropriate addition to the reward. Some dog trainers use food tidbits for this purpose, but it is not recommended here, except in special situations.

When a dog is being obedience-trained, he works for your praise as his reward. It tells him that you are pleased with his performance and reinforces the teaching of each command. German Shepherds work for your approval. Most Shepherds are high-energy, outgoing dogs, but not all. Some are moderate-tempered, somewhat insecure, less outgoing, or more sensitive than others.

High-energy Shepherds should be praised each time they carry out a command properly, but not to the extent that they become overly excited. If you are too enthusiastic with your praise, the dog will become extremely playful rather than attentive, and the training session will end. Moderate-tempered Shepherds should be praised with cheerfulness and enthusiasm to make them secure and less hesitant.

Corrections

There is only one acceptable way to communicate to your dog that he did the wrong thing, and that is with a *correction*. A correction is a reprimand conveyed to the dog in a way that is not harsh, abusive, or angry. It is simply a negative message that is communicated with a leash and training collar and with the word "NO." A leash correction (see The Corrective Jerk, page 114) and a verbal correction ("NO!") are usually given at the same time, although verbal corrections alone are all that is necessary for a trained dog.

All German Shepherds are sensitive and cannot tolerate severe corrections, harsh verbal reprimands, or punishments. They do vary to some degree in temperament and personality, however. Most Shepherds are high-energy dogs and require a firm leash correction followed by moderate praise because they want to play, run, and jump most of the time. There are Shepherds with moderate temperaments who respond best to softer, gentler corrections with highly enthusiastic praise. When training your own dog, you will quickly learn by trial and error how firm to make your corrections and how energetic your praise should be to get the appropriate response from the dog.

The Training Collar and Leash

Before you are able to administer a leash correction or teach any of the commands, you must know how to use the training collar and leash. This involves the correct way to place the collar around the dog's neck and learning how to hold the leash properly.

Placing the Training Collar around the Dog's Neck

Hold one end of the collar by the ring with your left hand. The length of chain will fall into a vertical line. Attach the leash to the top ring. Grasp the bottom ring with your right hand. Work the chain (or nylon) through the bottom ring so that it drops through, forming a wide loop. Gravity will help. Most of the chain will drop through the bottom ring, creating a loop that goes around the dog's neck like a lasso.

As you face the dog, place the loop around his neck. This must be done properly for the dog's comfort and to make the collar work correctly. *The collar must be capable of tightening around the dog's neck when pulled and loosening when released.* It must slide back and forth smoothly and quickly. This is essential.

When placing the training collar over the dog's head, it is correct if it resembles the letter *P* around his neck as you face him. It is incorrect if it resembles the number *9.* *(If the collar is put on incorrectly, it will not tighten and release quickly and smoothly.)*

Holding the Leash Properly

Stand next to the dog on his right side, facing in the same direction, so that you are both looking forward. At the end of every leather and nylon leash is a sewn loop serving as a handle. Hook the top of the loop onto your right thumb. As it hangs from your thumb across your palm, grab the middle of the leash with your left hand and fold it over the loop that is hooked around your right thumb. Four straps of leather now lie across the palm of your right hand. Close your fingers around them so they are pointing toward you. Adjust the length of the leash so that it crosses the width of your body, allowing a little slack.

For added strength, grip the leash with *both* hands as if holding a baseball bat. Place your left hand directly under the right one. This allows you to jerk the leash effectively when correcting your dog. Maintain a relaxed but firm grip. Keep your hands close to the center of your body, slightly above or below the waist (whichever is more comfortable). The grip described above gives you absolute control. Few dogs can bolt from you when held in this manner.

Draw a line with a pen on the middle portion of the leash where it loops over your thumb. This helps you find the right location each time you use the leash. Draw a second line on the sewn loop at the top of the leash to remind you to hook it onto your thumb.

The Corrective Jerk

The corrective jerk is used extensively throughout this course and is an integral part of it. This important teaching tool sends a signal to the dog in the most effective, direct manner that he did the wrong thing. The leash and training collar represent a line of communication that sends corrective signals to the dog. Using them properly is a significant aspect of obedience training and solving dog problems. However, the corrective jerk must be used only as a means of communication and not as a form of punishment. *Please note that young puppies should not wear training collars. They should be corrected gently with a leash and buckled collar.*

The corrective jerk is a correction involving a quick, gentle tug of the leash that tightens the training collar around the dog's neck for an instant. It sends an unmistakable, negative signal. If the trainer jerks the leash too hard, it is abusive and ineffective. If the trainer jerks the leash too softly, it communicates nothing to the dog. Administering the correction properly depends on the personality and temperament of the dog being taught. The point is to communicate a negative message; nothing more, nothing less.

Administering the Corrective Jerk

Stand to the right of the dog, facing in the same direction. Hold the leash as described above. Quickly jerk it to your right side in a horizontal direction. When jerking the leash, do it firmly, releasing the tension on the leash *immediately* following the jerk by returning your arms quickly to their original position. *This is very important.* Do not jerk the leash forward or in any direction other than to your right side.

The dog will feel the correction as the training collar tightens for an instant around his neck. It gives him an unmistakable signal that he performed incorrectly or that he did not listen to you. As you administer each leash correction, say, "NO," in a firm tone of voice and then follow it with verbal praise. *It is essential that you praise the dog immediately following each correction.*

The correction communicates to the dog that he did the wrong thing, and the praise reassures him that he is still accepted and loved as a member of the family. The praise is also given as a reward for accepting the correction. Your dog will work for your praise as his reward. Corrections and rewards reinforce the teaching process and effectively motivate the dog.

Do not practice leash corrections on your dog. They will confuse and upset him. All corrections must serve a purpose and be given for incorrect performance or misbehavior. Corrections must be fair.

"NO" and "OKAY"

"NO" is a verbal correction, and is an important training tool. When you correct a dog, it is important to say, "NO," with a firm, resonant sound to get the dog's attention and convince him that you mean business. The verbal correction is simply one word, "NO," but must never be hollered out in anger. When the correction "NO" is said properly, the dog should instantly stop whatever he is doing and totally accept your authority.

The corrective jerk must always be accompanied with the verbal correction "NO." However, the verbal correction "NO" does not always require the corrective jerk. Eventually "NO," stated firmly, will suffice without the need for any other correction.

"OKAY" is a positive-sounding command that gets a dog to anticipate forward movement or a release from discipline. Use it as a positive tag to your dog's name when giving him a command involving forward motion, such as "HEEL" or "COME." Example: "OKAY, Jason, COME!" It must always sound upbeat and happy.

"OKAY" is the ideal command for telling your dog that he is released from his training session or from a formal walk. After walking in HEEL, you may want to release your dog so that he can relieve himself. Simply say, "OKAY," and allow him to use the full length of the leash to get to the curb. "OKAY" should always be said in a happy, enthusiastic tone of voice with the emphasis on the *Oh*. Releasing your dog from a training session with this command should inspire the dog to prance with pleasure.

Leash Breaking

You cannot obedience-train a dog unless he is wearing a leash and collar. Some puppies resist wearing a leash for the first time. Leash breaking should begin soon after you bring your young dog home. Shepherds usually have no difficulty adjusting to the leash but, like all puppies, may resist wearing it for the first time because they do not want their movements to be restrained. The reaction to wearing a leash for the first time varies in puppies from immediate acceptance to stubborn refusal to fear. Some puppies bite the leash and try to pull it off with their paws.

Get your new dog to accept his leash by placing a buckled collar around his neck with a lightweight leash attached to it. Let him drag it around all day for several days. *(Never leave your dog, young or old, alone with a leash attached to his collar. Doing so could lead to a fatal accident.)*

The dog will probably adjust to wearing the leash and collar in one to three days. Be certain the buckled collar is comfortable. Always be cheerful and upbeat when attaching the leash to the collar. Create a pleasant association with it. Offer a food tidbit as you do this.

Entice the puppy to follow you and walk around the house while dragging the leash. After a while, pick up the leash and walk around with the dog. Stay relaxed and upbeat as though you were taking a casual stroll. As you hold the leash, entice the dog to walk with you in a playful manner, allowing as much slack as possible. Do this as often as possible for the entire leash-breaking period.

Once the dog has made an adjustment to the leash by wearing it around the house, especially with you holding it, try walking him outdoors. It is preferable to start out on a soft, grassy surface. If he resists walking with the leash, the grass will prevent his paws from being painfully scraped as they would be on a hard, rough sidewalk.

Many puppies refuse to walk when attached to a leash for the first time. They simply will not move. Sometimes they lean against a wall and refuse to move away from it. This is fear rather than stubbornness. If your puppy refuses to walk while attached to the leash, drop to your knees and call him to you in a very happy, cheerful tone of voice. Do not drag him, holler at him, or punish him in any way. Make him feel safe and loved. Try to create a pleasant association with the leash. When the little dog finally comes to you, praise him lavishly, stand up, and start to walk with him as you hold the leash with as much slack as possible.

It is common for a puppy to paw or bite the leash when having it placed around his neck for the first time. When that happens, give the dog a verbal correction. Say, "NO," in a mild but firm tone of voice and pull the leash away from him. It is essential to praise the dog enthusiastically immediately after each correction.

About the Command "SIT"

When given the command "SIT," your dog is expected to sit erect on his haunches. He must move into an upright position with his front legs straight and vertically extended in front of his body. The dog's attention should be fixed on his trainer.

Teaching SIT requires a training collar and a six-foot leather leash for an adolescent or adult dog. Young puppies should wear a buckle-type collar. Attach the leash to the collar and hold it with your right hand as previously instructed in The Corrective Jerk (page 114).

Work with a shortened leash by gathering up the slack in your right hand, allowing approximately one foot of it to remain between the collar and your left hand. With only a short length of leash available to the dog, you have all the control necessary for teaching the command.

Although German Shepherds want to please their owners, bear in mind that they are intelligent, strong-willed, territorial, protective, and dominant. It's as if your dog were thinking, "Okay, I'll do what you want and I'll try to please you, but it's not going to be easy."

When teaching the command "SIT," you must establish your dominance in the relationship. This is easily accomplished by the understanding that you are the teacher and your dog is the student. The key to success is to work with a firm, no-nonsense manner and tone of voice, but with love.

Teaching SIT to a high-energy Shepherd is difficult in the beginning because he will be fidgety and excitable. You have the option of training your dog indoors or outdoors, depending on his energy level. Select a quiet outdoor area with no one present or a small, quiet area of your home, such as a hallway. If indoors, place your dog against a wall so he cannot move to the left and out of your reach. Handle him with short-leash control, no more than one or two feet of leash.

You may teach SIT to a Shepherd of moderate temperament indoors or outdoors, with no spectators present. Moderate-tempered dogs require a very gentle, light touch. Be patient and calm, using mild corrections when necessary. Praise should be given with exuberance to a moderate-tempered dog. You may hug him and do anything that builds his confidence. Train him in a quiet place with no distractions. If the dog is fearful and lowers his head in submissiveness, try using motivational aids, such as food treats, a ball, or even a squeaky toy. The idea is to get the dog to look up at you as you teach the command. Praise, love, and affection are the most important tools for dogs of this temperament.

Teaching "SIT"

1. Start out on your dog's right side, facing in the same direction. Stand next to a high-energy dog or kneel on one knee next to a moderate-tempered dog. Hold approximately one foot of the leash taut over the dog's head with your right hand.

2. Hold the dog at the base of his spine (at the hip joints) with your left hand. You will feel two indentations. With a firm grip, press them gently with your fingers.

Hold the dog at the base of his spine (at the hip joints) with your left hand. You will feel two indentations. With a firm grip, press them gently with your fingers.

As you say the command, push the dog's rear end downward with your left hand as you pull the front of his body gently upward with the leash in your right hand.

3. Say the command, "S-I-I-I-T," stretching the word out as you say it. It is best to use a cheerful tone of voice that descends in tone as the dog moves down into position.

4. As you say the command, push the dog's rear end downward with your left hand while pulling the front of his body gently upward by the leash with your right hand.

Puppies and adult dogs alike learn this command easily and quickly and can be maneuvered into the proper position without difficulty. Once your dog is in SIT, tell him how smart he is, even though you placed him in the proper position. With repetition of the teaching steps, the dog will quickly learn SIT on command.

A high-energy dog may nip at you or mouth your hands or legs as you try to teach him this command. When he does, give him a quick leash correction and a firm "NO" the instant he misbehaves. Repeat the command "SIT" and then praise him. The praise should be moderate, because the more expressive you are with him, the more he is going to want to stop and play.

Once the dog understands what is expected of him, try giving the command without pushing him in place. Say, "SIT," and gently raise the leash with your right hand. Praise him each time he goes into the SIT position.

Next, eliminate pulling up the leash. Say, "SIT," and do not apply any hand or leash pressure. Praise the dog each time he obeys the command properly.

Try giving the command in different parts of the house and get him to obey without squirming around. Next, take the dog outdoors and give him the command. Once he performs properly outdoors, give him the command with more and more slack in the leash. The result should be that you can give the command "SIT" from six feet away from the dog, from the front of him, the side of him, from the back of him. When he can respond in all those situations, you can expose him to other animals as you give him the command.

As your dog becomes tired, end the session on a high note after the successful completion of the command. Allow the dog to have a bowl of water, to relieve himself, and to take a nap.

About the Command "SIT-STAY"

When given the command "STAY," your dog is expected to remain in the SIT position until released from the command. The dog's attention should be fixed on his trainer.

STAY is a difficult command for high-energy German Shepherds. They are fidgety dogs, constantly moving and looking around and eager to play. The command may be taught indoors or outdoors, depending on the energy level of your dog. Teach STAY in a quiet area, with no spectators present. If you train indoors, select a hallway to work in. That will enable you to box in a highly energetic dog with the wall at his back and a barrier on his left and right side. He'll have no choice but to remain in the SIT position without moving in any direction. Chairs on each side of the dog will serve as barriers. Whether working indoors or outdoors, in the beginning a quiet environment is important if the dog is expected to concentrate on what you teach him.

As you teach the dog, repeat the verbal commands often if your Shepherd is a high-energy type. Correct him with a firm but not harsh tone of voice. When you praise the dog, do not be too high-spirited or he will become excited and playful.

Moderate-tempered Shepherds have a much easier time with STAY because they will remain in one place, but for the wrong reason—insecurity. Use an open space, indoors, without barriers on the sides of the dog when teaching the command. Insecure dogs should be encouraged to be somewhat playful and outgoing. Praise dogs of this type with energy, exuberance, and an excited, high-pitched voice as if talking to a baby. Try whining like a puppy. Get the dog to enjoy the session by getting his attention and keeping it.

When teaching techniques involving side-to-side movements as the dog stays in place, use quick motions with a bounce to your step as you walk around him. Keep talking as you maneuver through the teaching process, repeating the command and congratulating the dog for staying in place. Never allow a moderate-tempered dog to become bored or uninterested.

Teaching SIT-STAY

The instructions for STAY involve a verbal command, a hand signal, and a special pivotal turn on the ball of your left foot.

1. With the dog on your left side, stand side by side, facing the same direction. Hold the leash in your right hand, with two or three feet draped across your knees. Give the command "SIT." If the dog does not obey, give him a leash correction at the same time, saying, "NO," in a firm but not harsh tone of voice. Praise the dog for the sake of reassurance. He should go into the proper position. Praise

The hand signal is given with the left hand as you hold the leash with your right hand.

him again. If he does not, go back to teaching SIT.

2. Next, say the command "STAY," and use the hand signal. The hand signal is given with the left hand as you hold the leash with your right hand. Flatten your left hand as if for a salute and place it in front of the dog's face with your palm facing his eyes. As you give the command "STAY," place your left hand four inches away from the front of his eyes. Do not touch the dog's eyes. The dog's vision should be blocked for only an instant. Place your left hand under your right hand, on the leash. Eventually the dog will remain in STAY with the use of the hand signal alone.

3. With both hands on the leash, make a pivotal turn on your left foot so that you end up facing the dog as he remains in the SIT-STAY position. To do this, swivel on the ball of your left foot as you slowly move the right foot in front of the dog. As the right foot moves in place, your body will turn with it. Slide your left foot over to your right so that they are slightly apart. You should now be facing the dog. Throughout the pivotal turn, you must keep holding the leash above his head to keep him in position. If you do this any other way, the dog will assume you are about to move forward and start to go with you.

The leash must be taut and held upward, to the side of the dog, so that it does not hit him on the chin. Leash control is the most important teaching element in this command. In a subdued tone of voice congratulate the dog for not moving (despite the fact that you held him in place with the leash). Repeat this step several times, keeping the dog in the STAY position for thirty seconds each time. Praise him for his accurate responses and correct him for his errors. The pivotal turn is merely a teaching tool and will not be used after the dog has learned the command thoroughly.

4. The next step is to teach the dog to remain in SIT-STAY as you stand in front of him from a distance of one, two, three, and six feet, until he is released from the command. This is a gradual process requiring diligence from the trainer as well as the dog.

From one foot away. Repeat steps 1, 2, and 3 until you are certain the dog will remain sitting in front of you while you are one foot away from him.

5. *From two feet away.* While still holding the leash above the dog's head, transfer it to your left hand, placing your thumb inside the loop at the very top. With your right hand, grasp the leash eighteen inches above the collar and hold it loosely. The leash must be able to slide through your right hand once you start to move away from the dog. The technique will eliminate any slack from developing as you move away. If the leash slackens, you will be unable to force the dog to remain in SIT-STAY.

While standing in front of the dog, back away approximately two feet, allowing the leash to extend but always in a taut position. The dog may try to move toward you. Say, "NO," as you quickly return to your original position by the dog's right side, praise him, and maintain a taut leash extended above the dog's head. Stand next to the dog once again and repeat steps 1, 2, and 3. Wait thirty seconds and try backing away again. Repeat this procedure until the dog finally holds his position from two feet away, for which you must praise him. Repeat the process until you feel the dog has learned the command at that distance.

6. *From three feet away.* Repeat steps 1, 2, and 3. As you back away from the dog, allow the leash to slide through your right hand as you hold it with the loop around the thumb of your left hand. As you move backward, keep the leash taut, allowing it to extend between you and the dog. Do not pull on the leash or the dog will walk toward you. If he does, repeat the command "STAY" in a firm tone of voice

and move in toward him, back to a distance of one foot. As you move forward, pull the leash through your right hand with your left hand and then hold it above his head as much as possible. In most instances the dog will stop moving as you take your first step toward him. If he does, praise him. Begin backing away again after several seconds, until you reach your goal of three feet in front of the dog. Praise him. Hold the position for thirty seconds. Repeat the process until you feel the dog has learned the command at that distance.

7. *From six feet away.* Do not attempt SIT-STAY from six feet until you are certain the dog can remain in position from the shorter distances. Always start out the session with the shorter distances. With that accomplished, proceed to six feet.

Repeat steps 1, 2, and 3. As before, slowly walk backward one step at a time. Command the dog "STAY," and praise him after each step. Use a firm but gentle tone of voice that is soft and soothing. Your tone of voice is important so as not to entice the dog to move toward you. Bear in mind that you no longer have the same level of leash control at this distance. As you back away, the dog is quite likely to run to you. If that happens, give him the command "STAY" and step forward to block him, shortening the leash quickly by sliding it through your right hand as you pull it with your left hand. Hold it taut above his head. Give him the command "SIT." As he obeys, praise him, wait a few seconds, and back slowly away until you reach the full extent of the six-foot leash. Remain standing in front of him for thirty seconds so he absorbs the meaning of STAY. Return to your original position and repeat all the steps until you are satisfied that the dog has successfully learned to obey the command from six feet.

8. *Walking around the dog.* You are now ready to teach your dog to hold the position as you walk around each side of him and then walk around him in a complete circle.

Repeat steps 1, 2, and 3. Walk halfway around the dog's right side from two feet in front of him. Remember to hold the leash taut above his head. Return quickly to the front position. Do it several times. Once he tolerates that movement without leaving his position, try walking around to his left side and returning. With that accomplished, walk a complete circle around the dog as he holds his STAY position. As you succeed in these motions, increase the distance, as in the earlier steps, until you can walk completely around the dog from six feet away.

Once the dog obeys sufficiently to hold his position as you walk around him from six feet, move in front of him and turn your back to him. Your dog has completely mastered the command SIT-STAY when you can command him to SIT and then STAY.

End each training session on a happy note of success.

About the Command "HEEL" and the Automatic SIT

HEEL

"HEEL" means your dog must walk with you on command, paying attention so that he keeps pace with you, turns with you, and never pulls ahead or lags behind. The dog must stay on your left side, keeping his head even with your left leg, and stop when you stop.

Teaching this breed any command can turn into a battle of wills. To offset this, you must establish your dominance in the relationship. This is easily accomplished by the understanding that you are the teacher and your dog is the student. The key to success is to work with a firm, no-nonsense manner and tone of voice, but with love.

A high-energy Shepherd is going to be distracted by anything and everything when you try to teach him the command "HEEL." As you start out, the dog will run to the end of the leash, pulling with excitement. He will run in all directions, bouncing to the left, bouncing to the right, jumping all over the place. To bring your dog under control, train him in a quiet area where there are no distractions or spectators. Once the dog has mastered the command, you may practice in a busy area to test his ability to obey.

When rewarding a high-energy dog with verbal praise for obeying properly, do not be too exuberant. Modify your tone of voice so that he doesn't become excited and jump all over you, making it impossible to go on with the lesson. Give him just enough encouragement to perform properly and want to be with you. You may lavish praise on him at the end of each training session.

The moderate-tempered Shepherd, whether he is shy, unsure of himself, reserved, or simply hesitant, will probably walk behind you in the beginning. He may cling to you or trot hesitantly by your side. Sensitive dogs such as these should be given mild leash corrections, and not too many of them. These dogs should also be trained in a quiet area with no distractions or spectators. Once the dog has mastered the command, you may practice in a busy area to test his ability to obey.

When praising moderate-tempered dogs, use a high-pitched tone of voice that is playful and friendly. Every time you pause during the teaching sessions, kneel down to the dog's level and praise him affectionately. If you constantly stand over the dog, towering above him, you will cultivate a submissive personality. Encourage him with hugs, kisses, and praise to give him confidence in you and in himself. Unlike the high-energy dog, he can even be allowed to jump on you to make him more outgoing.

Be very physical in your movements when teaching this command. Make quick and sudden turns, changing your pace frequently, walking slowly one minute and fast the next. Try to motivate moderate-tempered dogs and get them to walk close to you. Try using squeak toys, balls, or even food treats if that's what it takes to bring the dog out of his shell. The more you express loving playfulness, the quicker the dog will learn to walk in HEEL.

Limit each training session to fifteen minutes and conduct no more than two a day, spaced at least four hours apart. However, you may practice walking in HEEL many times during the day, especially if you have an errand to run. Practice walking in HEEL when you take your dog out to relieve himself. The more you practice, the sooner the dog will master the command.

As you say the word "HEEL," step forward with your left foot.

Teaching the Command "HEEL"

High-energy dogs require firm corrections and subdued praise. Moderate-tempered Shepherds require mild corrections, playful coaxing, and energized praise.

1. With the dog at your left side, attach the training collar and six-foot leather leash, as described earlier. Both arms should dangle at your sides in a relaxed position. Hold the leash at the halfway mark with your right hand and allow the remaining half to drape across your knees, hooked onto the dog's collar.

2. Give your dog the command "SIT," and praise him if he obeys. Next, give the command "STAY," using the appropriate hand signal. Hold the leash in your right hand in the normal manner, ready to correct the dog if necessary. Once again, praise him if he obeys properly.

3. In the verbal command for HEEL, the dog's name is said first, followed by the word "HEEL." "HEEL" is a forward-motion command, and the dog's name is what gets his attention, along with the movement of your left foot. "HEEL" is a command that propels your dog into forward motion. His name is actually a signal getting him ready to move forward.

Say, "George, HEEL." As you say the word "HEEL," step forward with your left foot. It is closest to the dog's line of sight and will get him moving the instant you step off. The first thing your high-energy dog will do is run ahead of you.

4. Just before the dog reaches the end of the leash, make a very firm right U-turn and stride in the opposite direction. This may take a great deal of strength, depending on the dog. As you begin your turn, say, "George, HEEL," in a loud, firm tone of voice. The dog will be stopped suddenly from running ahead and forced to move quickly to catch up with you. In effect, he will have corrected himself. Keep walking briskly in the opposite direction. This turn of events comes as an abrupt surprise to the dog. He has no choice but to keep up with you or feel the force of the leash pulling him in your direction. In the most definite sense, this action establishes you in the dominant, yet loving, position. It is the first time that you really begin to gain control over the dog. You will be imposing your will over his impulsive desires.

5. As the dog tries to catch up with you, tap your left leg in a friendly manner and invite him to get closer. Try to get him to position his head next to your leg. Praise him as he gets near you.

6. If your dog runs past you again, repeat the right U-turn procedure and keep repeating it until the dog learns to keep pace with you and maintain the proper position. With each repetition, the dog will walk closer and closer to you, and eventually will walk with you, in the proper position, keeping his head next to your left leg.

Whenever the dog fails to maintain the correct HEEL position, administer a leash correction. Gently jerk the leash to your right and say, "George, HEEL," execute a U-turn, and walk in the opposite direction. Praise a high-energy dog in a subdued manner, and a moderate-tempered dog with enthusiasm and exuberance.

Shy, sensitive Shepherds tend to lag behind or go off to the left or cling to your leg. Do not give your dog too many leash corrections. Rely more on enticement with your voice and friendly body language. Walk slowly, change your pace, run, walk faster, make many quick turns. Sensitive Shepherds are not going to want to be at the end of the leash and must be motivated to keep up. Balls, squeak toys, gentle tugs of the leash, and even food tidbits are desirable motivators. The trick is to get the dog to walk close to you without a lot of leash corrections.

Talking to your sensitive dog or young puppy is the best answer. Playfully encourage him to catch up and keep pace. The happy sound of your voice can make all the difference.

If necessary, kneel and call the dog to you. When he reaches you, rise quickly and begin walking in the same direction. If the dog or puppy does not respond properly, you may gently snap the leash with a slight jerk or pull. What is desirable is to keep the dog focused on you.

Automatic SIT

Every time the dog walks in HEEL, he must stop when you stop and SIT without being given a command. After being given the command "STAY" (and then being praised), he must hold his position until he is released or given the next command, which is usually "HEEL."

This command is accomplished by communicating to the dog that you are going to stop walking. You simply slow down before coming to a halt. Slowing down as you walk is a signal to the dog to be ready to stop and SIT, automatically, once you stop moving forward. This is one of the reasons it is important for the dog to stay focused on you when walking in HEEL.

Teaching Automatic SIT

1. Begin the lesson by placing the dog in the SIT-STAY position.
2. Give the command, "Jason, HEEL" (praise the dog immediately after giving the command), and walk in HEEL for at least one minute at a moderate speed. Gradually slow down until you finally stop walking.
3. Give the dog the command "SIT." If he obeys, as he should by now, reward him with praise. Remember, high-energy dogs must be given praise in a subdued tone of voice, while moderate-tempered dogs must be praised with exuberance.
4. If the dog does not respond properly to the command, say, "NO," in a firm tone of voice and administer a corrective jerk by tugging the leash upward and to the right side, immediately following up

with praise. If he was taught SIT properly, the dog should obey the command after the correction. If he still does not respond properly, say, "SIT," and follow with another leash correction to reinforce the command. If the dog does not respond to this, you must return to Teaching SIT (page 118) and teach the command all over again. Once the dog obeys the command and places himself in the SIT position on command, praise him in the appropriate manner.

5. Getting the dog to sit automatically after walking in HEEL is the result of repeating the above procedure for at least twenty minutes, several times a day, Give the dog a break after each ten minutes of repetition and finish the lesson after the next ten minutes. End the session by saying, "OKAY," in a happy tone of voice, allow the dog to relieve himself, and then happily walk home.

6. Practice this command every day until the dog sits automatically after walking in HEEL without being commanded to do it.

About the Commands "DOWN" and "DOWN-STAY"

DOWN

The command "DOWN" is given verbally and with a hand signal. On command, the dog must lower himself to the ground, where he remains with his head erect and his front legs extended forward. He may lower his head and place his chin on the ground if he must remain in position for more than a few minutes.

Despite the fact that German Shepherds want to please their owners they also want to be "top dog." Bear in mind that they are intelligent, strong-willed, territorial, protective, and dominant. It may not be easy.

When teaching the command "DOWN," you must establish your dominance in the relationship. This is easily accomplished by the understanding that you are the teacher and your dog is the student. The key to success is to work with a firm, no-nonsense manner and tone of voice, but with love.

This is the most difficult command for any dog to learn and accept. DOWN is the ultimate position of subordination. It also demands of the dog that he obey the command and control his instinct to react impulsively to anything that stimulates him. For these reasons, it is important to begin the training of high-energy or moderate-tempered Shepherds in a quiet, indoor area with no one else present and with as few distractions as possible.

Because the dog's front legs initially must be slid into position when being taught this command, the surface of the floor is an important consideration. The best surface is linoleum because of its smoothness. Other surfaces, especially carpet, create friction, which could be painful, when sliding the dog into the DOWN position. A smooth surface also allows the command to be taught with far less effort.

Two teaching techniques are offered here for the first part of this command. The first one, the *push-and-pull technique*, is suited for high-energy Shepherds. The second one, the *sweep technique*, is best for moderate-tempered Shepherds. After teaching either one of these techniques, you must go on to teach the remaining aspects of the command, which involve the *hand technique* and the *front technique*.

The verbal command. When saying the command word "DOWN," extend the middle portion of the word so that is it spoken in a longer, exaggerated way. The sound you make should start at a high point and get lower and lower as you reach the end of the word: "DOWWwwnnnn." It is like music to a dancer and will help the dog move properly to the sound of your voice. As your voice descends in tone, it should inspire your dog to do the same with his body.

The hand signal. This important aspect of the command is taught when the dog is placed in the DOWN position by applying pressure on the extended training collar with your hand. This part of the teaching occurs in the hand technique and the front technique.

The hand signal requires that you flatten your left hand as if for a military salute as you face the dog. Raise your left arm fully above your head. Say the command "DOWWwwnnnn" and lower your left arm at a steady rate of movement so that the dog sees it coming down. The objective is to associate your lowering arm with the command "DOWN." Once this is accomplished, you will be able to stand a good distance from the dog and simply give him the hand signal, to which he will respond as he should. Praise him after each command and signal is given.

Teaching DOWN with the Push-and-Pull Technique (for High-Energy Shepherds)

1. Place the dog on your left side, with both of you facing in the same direction. Hold the leash properly with both hands and do not allow any slack in it. (See Holding the Leash Properly, page 113.) Say, "SIT," and praise the dog for obeying. Say, "STAY," using the hand signal described in Teaching "SIT-STAY" (page 121). Praise the dog again.

2. Kneel next to the dog's right side and place the leash in your left hand. You will have better control of the dog if you take up all the slack in the leash so that you can hold him in position if necessary.

3. Place your left hand (with the leash in it) on the dog's shoulder, just below the neck, gripping it with your thumb and middle finger. Take hold of the dog's right front leg just above the paw.

4. Say the command "DOWWwwnnnn" and push the dog's shoulder downward with your left hand as you lift his right leg, pulling it forward and slightly out to the right side. These combined actions get the dog into a DOWN position on the ground. If the dog tends to favor his left leg as he stands, then pull his left leg out instead. Keep the leash as taut as possible as the dog moves downward. Praise him for going into the DOWN position, even though you placed him there.

5. Once the dog is DOWN, you may hold him in that position for ten seconds by placing your foot on the leash. Otherwise, he will jump out of position instantly.

6. Repeat this procedure ten or fifteen times, until the dog offers little or no resistance to being placed in DOWN. Some dogs go into the proper position on command without being placed there at this

stage of the teaching. Most do not. You may end the session here and practice these steps several times a day until the next lesson.

You are now ready to continue on to the next step, which is the hand technique, skipping the following sweep technique for moderate-tempered Shepherds.

It is important to understand that this technique is only the first step when teaching DOWN. After teaching the push-and-pull technique you must continue with the hand technique and the front technique. These are essential.

Teaching DOWN with the Sweep Technique (for Moderate-Tempered Shepherds)

1. Place the dog on your left side, with both of you facing in the same direction. Hold the leash properly with both hands and do not allow any slack in it. (See Holding the Leash Properly, page 113.) Say, "SIT," and praise the dog for obeying. Say, "STAY," using the hand signal described in Teaching SIT-STAY (page 121). Praise the dog again.

2. Kneel next to the dog's right side and place the leash in your left hand. You will have better control of the dog if you take up all the slack in the leash so that you can hold him in position if necessary.

3. Place your right hand behind the dog's front legs, near his belly.

4. In a firm voice say, "DOWWwwnnnn," in the exaggerated manner recommended for the verbal command (page 132). Given the sensitive nature of moderate-tempered Shepherds, your voice should be gentle, soothing, firm but loving.

5. As you say the command "DOWWwwnnnn," glide your right hand under the dog's belly toward his chest, moving his legs upward and to the front so that he must gently go into the DOWN position. As the dog's legs move off the ground, keep your right hand in motion until he is in the DOWN position. Praise your dog each time you do this.

6. Repeat these steps ten or fifteen times, or until the dog offers

no resistance to being placed in the DOWN position. He may begin to go into DOWN without being placed in position by the end of this teaching step. You may end the session here and practice several times a day until the next training lesson.

You are now ready to continue on to the next step, the hand technique.

Teaching DOWN with the Hand Technique (for High-Energy and Moderate-Tempered Shepherds)

Whether you used the push-and-pull technique or the sweep technique to maneuver the dog into the DOWN position, you must now add the use of your hand as part of the teaching process. This phase of the command is necessary for teaching the dog to respond to the hand signal without a command.

1. Place the dog on your left side, with both of you facing in the same direction. Hold the leash properly with both hands and do not allow any slack in it. Say, "SIT," and praise the dog for obeying. Say, "STAY," using the hand signal described in Teaching Sit-Stay (page 121). Praise the dog again.

2. Kneel next to the dog's right side. Hold the leash with your right hand across your chest and keep it taut. On a tight leash, he can do nothing but SIT. Flatten your left hand as if for a military salute. Raise your left arm above your head.

3. Say the command "DOWWwwnnnn" and lower your left arm so that the dog can see it coming down past his eyes and onto the top of the taut leash where the clip attaches to the training collar. By now the dog should be lowering his body in response to the verbal command.

4. While you are still saying "DOWWwwnnnn," your left hand should be pressing the leash all the way to the ground. Praise the dog as he reaches the ground.

5. Repeat this procedure at least fifteen times. The objective is for the dog to associate your lowering hand with the command "DOWN." With this accomplished, you will eventually be able to give the hand signal alone for DOWN from a good distance away and get him to

obey the command. If the dog does not respond properly or resists this part of the lesson, place him in SIT-STAY and begin again. You may end the session here, but you must practice this technique several times a day until the next training lesson.

Teaching DOWN with the Front Technique (for High-Energy and Moderate-Tempered Shepherds)

The front technique is the next logical step for teaching DOWN. This step familiarizes the dog with the hand signal as it will be used in the future and indoctrinates him to responding to it properly.

Lower your left arm so that the dog can see it coming down, past his eyes and onto the top of the taut leash where the clip attaches to the training collar.

Repeat the "DOWN" command from gradually increasing distances, until your dog obeys from the distance of the fully extended leash.

Now that the dog has learned to be pushed into DOWN with your hand on the leash from the side, it is safe to assume that you can accomplish the same thing from the front. Your dog's proper response to the hand signal is an important step in reinforcing his understanding of the entire command.

1. Hold the leash properly in your right hand and place the dog in SIT-STAY using the appropriate hand signal.

2. Pivot around on the ball of your left foot so that you stand directly in front of the dog, about two feet away from him. Switch the leash to your left hand. Hold it taut and as high above the dog's head as possible without bending your body forward.

3. Raise your right hand as high as you can, with your fingers extended straight and close to one another.

4. Say, "DOWWwwnnnn." As you give the command, lower your right hand in a steady, deliberate manner onto the leash. Push the top of the leash hard with your right hand, pressing it downward toward the ground. This teaches the dog to associate your lowering hand signal with the "DOWN" command and to comply with it. Elongate the verbal command "DOWWwwnnnn" until the dog is actually in the proper DOWN position.

5. If your dog lowers himself into DOWN without being pushed into position with the pressure of your descending hand, praise him enthusiastically and then repeat the exercise fifteen times. It is important to praise the dog the instant he is all the way down each time. Remember, the dog works for the praise. It is his motivation to please you. This is an appropriate place to end the session. Practice this step several times a day until the next training lesson.

The very next stage is to teach the front technique from greater distances. Simply repeat all five steps of the front technique in the following sessions but move farther away from the dog each time. Repeat the five steps from three feet away. After the dog succeeds from three feet, move to four feet, and so on, until he obeys from the fully extended leash, six feet. If you are ambitious, you may tie a long clothesline to the end of the leash and continually train the dog from even greater distances.

Once the dog responds properly from greater distances, the next phase is to repeat the front technique but without pushing or even touching the leash with your hand as you lower your arm. Allow your hand to brush past the leash without actually touching it. This will be exactly the way your hand signal will look from a distance. Repeat this phase until the dog obeys the command "DOWN" perfectly from your verbal command only and then from a hand signal only.

Teaching DOWN-STAY

To teach DOWN-STAY, return to the SIT-STAY lesson in this chapter and follow it completely. The only difference is to place the dog in DOWN wherever it instructs you to place the dog in SIT.

"DOWN-STAY" means your dog remains in the DOWN position on the ground or on the floor until you release him from the command. It is similar to SIT-STAY except that the dog goes into a DOWN position. The teaching techniques are identical to those of SIT-STAY. If the dog now responds properly to SIT-STAY, it can be assumed that he will have no difficulty learning DOWN-STAY. STAY in the DOWN position may confuse some dogs and they will require further teaching of the command, but it will be more of a refresher course. In that instance, repeat the teaching steps of SIT-STAY until the dog responds properly. Then continue on to DOWN-STAY using the same teaching techniques.

About the Command "*COME WHEN CALLED*"

On command, your dog must instantly stop whatever he is doing and come running to you quickly. When he arrives at your feet, he must go into a SIT position. The sequence involves a verbal command and a hand signal.

The foundation for this command is your dog's anticipation of pleasure when answering your call. A young Shepherd should fly to you with delight when you call him, provided that you have never scolded him when he got to you. If you have always clapped your hands happily and praised your dog when he came to you since the day you brought him home, then teaching this command will be much easier. Why would a dog (or a person) run to anyone only to be hollered at, hit, or disciplined?

It is not too late to create this feeling in your dog if you hug him and tell him how wonderful he is after you call him. Always be enthusiastic when he gets to you, and give him a lot of praise. The best possibility for teaching this command successfully is to make coming to you a very pleasant event.

The high-energy Shepherd

Teaching COME WHEN CALLED to this type of Shepherd can be great fun, considering the joyful enthusiasm of the breed. The problem, however, is how his energy level affects his responses to you. Some dogs are easily distracted and will promptly lose their focus and concentration. Another problem is calling the untrained dog to you. He will make a mad dash in your general direction, zigzagging along the way, and end up crashing into your legs. Sometimes it is funny and sometimes it is painful.

At the start, teach COME WHEN CALLED in a quiet indoor environment, with no distractions and no audience. You may move the lessons to a closed-in outdoor area with some distractions once the dog has learned the basics of the command and responds appropriately to them.

At the start of this command, use only two feet of the six-foot leash. It will give you more control over the dog while teaching the command. The more control you have when teaching the command, the quicker the dog will learn. A Shepherd will always come to you when you call him. However, a well-trained Shepherd will come straight to you and sit properly in front of you wherever you are standing. Critical leash control will accomplish that.

The training environment should be indoors, in a long hallway, so the dog will learn from the beginning to move toward you in a straight line. Set up a chute so the dog cannot veer to the left or right but must move straight to you when you call him. You can improvise a chute with anything: a wall and several chairs, two long benches, long planks of wood, a dog run, et cetera. An improvised chute will get a high-energy dog to focus on moving directly to you as you teach the command. Don't forget to praise the dog when he reaches you.

When praising the dog, use a moderate tone of voice that is not too high in pitch; otherwise, he will become excited. The most important elements are firm leash control and knowing exactly where you want your dog to be when he gets to you.

As you call the dog, move backward quickly so you can make adjustments with the leash and training collar and guide the dog into a straight line directly in front of you. The secret to teaching this command is positioning the dog properly as he comes to you.

An important aspect of this command is teaching the dog to go into a SIT position once he reaches you. In the beginning, however, do not worry about a high-energy Shepherd sitting properly as he gets to you. It is more important that he come to you on command. If you are too critical, you may discourage him from responding to your call. The first part of the command is getting the dog to come to you, and the second part is getting him to SIT properly.

The moderate-tempered Shepherd

A more reserved, sensitive Shepherd must be motivated to come to you on command. Use a fifteen- or thirty-foot leash (clothesline will do) so that the dog has a longer distance to get to you as you move backward. He may resist a six-foot leash when it is pulled. During the teaching process, try moving backward quickly as the dog comes toward you. This may energize the dog or at least appeal to his playfulness. Use a high-pitched tone of voice oozing with exuberance. Motivational aids such as balls, squeak toys, whistles, or any attention-getters are useful if they can get the dog to come to you without fear or hesitation.

Sometimes you can get a dog of this type to run to you by arous-

ing his curiosity with distractions that are just behind you, such as a
toy, another dog, or even another person.

Always keep the dog on-leash as you work outdoors, in a safe,
fenced-off area, just in case he bolts and you lose control of him. Do
not teach this command outdoors if the dog is off-leash. Off-leash
training is not part of this course and can be hazardous if not performed correctly.

Throughout the life of your moderate-tempered Shepherd, it is
important that he associate your call with a happy experience. If you
call him and then correct him, he will stop coming to you. Never call
your dog to correct his misbehavior. If you need to correct him, *always go to him.*

Teaching COME WHEN CALLED

The verbal command. COME WHEN CALLED requires three
words, "OKAY, Solly, COME." Each of the three words is a separate
part of the command.

Draw out the *ohhh* when you say, "*OHHH-KAY,*" and place the ac-
cent on the *Oh*. Raise the pitch of your voice so it sounds cheerful.
The word "OKAY" will create a feeling of pleasant anticipation in
your dog if it is said in a happy, upbeat tone.

The dog's name is meant to prepare him for forward motion. Let
your voice rise and say the name cheerfully.

"COME" is the actual command word. It tells him exactly what
you want him to do and therefore must be said with conviction and
emphasis.

Call your dog in the same way every time: "OKAY, Solly, COME!"
Always give the command for COME WHEN CALLED in this precise manner and have the other members of your family do so as well.
The hand signal. The verbal command is always given with a hand
signal. It eliminates confusion when calling the dog from a distance.
The right arm leaves the side of the body and is raised upward,
swinging to the left, toward the left shoulder. It is the same gesture
used to call someone to you.

The verbal command "COME" is always taught with a hand signal.

   1. Repeat all the commands the dog has learned up to this point.

   2. Place your dog in a SIT-STAY position. With only two feet of slack, hold the leash in your left hand and step in front of the dog, facing him.

   3. Say, "OKAY, Solly, COME."

   4. Do two things as you say, "OKAY." Motion the dog to come to you by quickly swinging your extended right arm around to your chest and gently tug on the leash with your left hand. Finish the command, "Solly, COME." You have just given the verbal command and the hand signal.

   5. The dog should move forward as you say the command and tug the leash. As soon as you have given the hand signal, place your right hand on the leash and, along with your left hand in a hand-over-hand motion, reel the leash in like a fishing line. As the dog reaches you, the leash should be gathered in your hands. Praise the dog for coming to you.

   6. Repeat these five steps at least fifteen times. If he does not

move toward you, add more excitement to the tone of your voice. If he does, praise him. Most dogs will respond properly.

The next phase of COME WHEN CALLED is teaching your dog to SIT once he reaches you, after obeying the first part of the command. The effect is to break up the teaching process into three separate stages, COME, SIT, and STAY. Do not forget to praise the dog after he obeys each of these commands.

1. Repeat the first six steps for teaching COME WHEN CALLED.

2. Place the dog in SIT-STAY. Praise him.

3. Command him to COME. Praise him.

4. Command him to SIT. Praise him.

5. Command him to STAY. Praise him.

6. Repeat each of these steps until the dog goes into a proper SIT position every time he comes to you on command.

COME WHEN CALLED concludes this *basic* obedience course for German Shepherds. By following these instructions, you will definitely be able to control your dog and enrich the quality of your relationship. It should be noted, however, that obedience training can go much further than the course offered here.

Dog obedience training is a sophisticated hobby, sport, and socially important function. The six obedience commands taught here are only an introduction to this important activity.

German Shepherds of all ages should maintain a high state of discipline with continuing education and refresher courses. Certainly, practicing all that was learned from this chapter on a continuing basis will keep you and your dog happy.

We encourage you to continue your dog's education with a more complete dog training book; by entering a training class; by engaging the services of a professional dog trainer; or by joining a club focused on the sport of obedience trials, many of which are sponsored by the American Kennel Club and the United Kennel Club.

Training a dog is satisfying and rewarding. Training a dog is also fun.

◆ ◆ ◆

German Shepherd Behavior Problems

Puppy owners believe that everything about their new dog is cute and adorable . . . and it is. The mischief of a new puppy can be entertaining and endearing. Misbehavior is usually seen as comical, lovable, and certainly excusable in a puppy. A little dog's negative behavior is thought of as frisky and does not seem very important until a month or two into the relationship, when the honeymoon is over. As the dog grows bigger and cannot be carried around like a baby, and when he nips a little harder and mouths objects, the dog owner's attitude begins to change. As a puppy grows, its behavior problems grow—and the family starts to panic. The ability to cope becomes more difficult. The cute behaviors of an eight-pound puppy lose their charm when they are seen in an eighty-pound dog.

German Shepherds are very oral, especially as puppies. If given the opportunity, they will happily chew on your books (hardcovers seem to taste best) or anything else they can gnaw on, including a stack of envelopes with your monthly bills and payments inside. They especially enjoy the flavor of rare books and record albums—the more expensive, the better. Compact discs and videotapes are high on the list of delicacies.

As puppies they will nip your fingers and mouth anything. They like to dig. It doesn't matter whether you have a splendid lawn, an unpaved backyard, or just a small patch of grass on the side of the house; most Shepherds can be counted on to dig holes into the entire surface. And they especially like to jump on you if you are wearing a white outfit or a spotless suit just back from the dry cleaner.

The new owner will be relieved to know that most of the behavior problems of German Shepherds can be avoided with prevention techniques and mild corrections employed as early as possible. Any behavior pattern exhibited by a puppy should be evaluated by the owner, who must consider whether it will be acceptable when the dog becomes an adult. For example, a cute eight-week-old puppy jumping on its owner's knee to be petted or picked up may not be so cute when it is a fully grown dog with smudgy paws. A new owner must show foresight when raising a puppy or spend the next twelve years correcting behavior that could have been easily avoided.

The various social behavior problems of the German Shepherd Dog are not addressed in this book. The subject is far too great for the focus of this guide. A detailed, in-depth treatment of the subject would be required, and such a study is beyond the scope of this guide.

The problem behavior of German Shepherd Dogs can be divided into two categories to make it easier to understand. The first category is behavior problems, which consist of those we write about in this chapter: excessive barking, chewing, digging, jumping on people, mouthing, and nipping. Every dog has these problems, or some of them.

The second category is social behavior problems, which involve unacceptable or dangerously aggressive behavior toward people, dogs, and other animals. It is seen in the form of intimidating body language, growling, lunging, or biting. In some instances certain aspects of this behavior are understandable if a German Shepherd Dog is encouraged or trained to protect his home and family. He is expected to ward off "bad guys." The problem is, it is often impossible for the dog to tell the "good guys" from the "bad guys." If it is left up to the dog to decide whom to bite, he will invariably become an indiscriminate biter. This is a problem for any large, working breed. The problem is determined by what the dog owner wants and doesn't want.

There are many reasons why a German Shepherd will have social behavior problems, some of which have to do with temperament, personality, shyness, fear-aggression, dominance-aggression, lack of socialization, owner abuse, and various other aspects of inherited and environmental influences.

At eight weeks of age the typical puppy is a happy, outgoing, and friendly animal. One must ask, "What happened?" in the case of dogs with social problems. Such behavior is almost always caused by bad breeding and indiscriminate breeding, especially from the puppy mills that stock pet shops. Another cause of social problems is the lack of proper socialization that is crucial in the first eight weeks to three months of the dog's life.

If you consider why some German Shepherds will be happy, loving dogs who in an instant will defend their territory to the death or become dangerous biters, you must examine a number of serious factors. Look beyond the dog himself. You must examine how he's been raised and the environment in which he's been brought up. Has he been allowed to be social with a variety of people and other dogs? Or was he deliberately left outdoors on his own?

Is he a genetic misfit (shy, insecure, overaggressive)? Was he raised with dogs exclusively, rather than with people? Was he raised by his owner with a one-dog, one-owner mentality and kept away from or made suspicious of anyone not in his immediate family? These are the issues that must be addressed when considering the social behavior problems of some German Shepherds. An untrained dog with the usual behavior problems in addition to these social problems is more than most people can handle.

When you live with a German Shepherd, you should be most concerned with developing a dog with a healthy social attitude and one that is friendly and loving to everybody. A German Shepherd in the hands of the wrong owner becomes a serious problem dog. This creates an undeserved bad reputation for the entire breed.

The most common, easily resolved behavior problems of German Shepherd Dogs are *(excessive) barking, chewing, digging, jumping on people, mouthing,* and *nipping.* Here are suggestions for solving these problems.

(Excessive) Barking

Most dogs bark. It is only considered a problem when a dog barks excessively. All German Shepherds will bark excessively if this behavior is tolerated and not corrected as soon as possible. German Shepherds have a natural tendency to bark to excess because of their natural protective characteristics of alertness and strong territorial feelings. Owners often tend to encourage their Shepherd to bark because they want a watchdog. When a dog is encouraged to bark, it inevitably leads to the problem of excessive barking.

Excessive barking, especially from a large, loud dog, is irritating not only to you but to your neighbors. As a dog owner, you must become a good neighbor, and your dog must become a canine good citizen. Many barking complaints are taken to court by angry neighbors, costing a great deal of time, money, and emotion. It's easier to work on the barking problem, especially if your dog is very young.

Reasons for the Problem

Improper confinement. Excessive barking often begins in puppyhood, when the untrained dog is not housebroken and has other problems, such as chewing. When he or she must leave the house or apartment, the owner unwisely places the small dog behind a closed door. Improper confinement will definitely cause a barking problem in addition to any other behavior problems. If the housebreaking or chewing problem had been dealt with properly, the barking problem would not have developed.

Being tied up. Indoors or outdoors, a tethered dog will sooner or later become frustrated and begin to bark to communicate his displeasure.

Outside distractions. When a dog is kept outside, he is likely to bark excessively at kids who tease him; at a steady stream of strangers (working and hunting breeds become very vocal in this situation); at a variety of street noises, including automobile backfires, firecrackers, and lawnmowers; at free-roaming dogs (strays and neighborhood dogs); and at the dog next door (who can create barking conversations).

Time of day. Some dogs will not bark during the day, because they have become accustomed to the daytime noises. In the warmer states many dog owners keep their dogs out overnight because it avoids hygiene and grooming problems inside the home, such as shedding fur and dirt. It is also a way of avoiding training and behavior problems. However, the dog is quite likely to start barking at two in the morning at the slightest sound, movement, or noise.

Overaggressiveness. All aspects of an aggressive dog's behavior can stimulate a long siege of unpleasant barking.

Strong territorial feelings. If there is no restraint or limitation placed on a territorial dog, he will bark excessively whenever a stranger enters your property, whether you're there or not, whether it's an invited guest or visitor on lawful business.

Temperament. Dogs of extreme temperaments will express their feelings by barking. Nervous, fear-ridden, and, in some cases, shy dogs will bark excessively at the slightest stimulation.

Solutions for Excessive Barking

Barking outdoors. If your dog and your neighbor's dog participate in "fence fighting" through a chain-link fence, it is important to prevent them from seeing each other. This can be accomplished by running pliable slats through the links; boarding up the fence completely; covering the fence with green, fine-mesh tennis netting; or placing the dog on the quiet side of the house, with a newly constructed dog run. You can purchase a portable dog run or a clothesline run that operates as an overhead trolley. Attach a clothesline eight or ten feet off the ground from the side of your house to a tree. Run the loop of a leash through the clothesline and attach it to your dog's collar. Be sure it's long enough to allow him to lie down. While this prevents the dog from gaining free access to that portion of the yard where he engages in barking duels with the dog next door, it gives him some freedom to move about the yard. You might calm a barking dog by appealing to his denning instinct, with a doghouse. You can easily build or purchase one. Check the various mail-order catalogs or talk to your hardware store dealer.

Perhaps your dog barks because he is thirsty or hungry. A hungry or thirsty dog will certainly complain in the only manner he knows. He'll bark or he'll chew. Reevaluate the dog's feeding schedule. If you're not home, perhaps a friend or neighbor could feed the dog a little later in the day. Be certain that no other animal is eating his daily food ration. A second dog, stray dogs, cats, squirrels, chipmunks, or even birds will eat any food they can find. This would certainly be the problem if your dog has the habit of turning his bowl on its side and spilling the food onto the ground. Use a heavy weighted bowl or feed the dog indoors, making certain that he has eaten his fill before he goes out in the yard on his own. You can purchase a self-feeder that provides dog food automatically with the help of a mechanical timer. You may provide cold water all day with a product called Lixit, which attaches to your outdoor faucet.

Do not keep a dog outdoors to avoid behavior problems, such as housebreaking or chewing. You may be trading one behavior problem for another. Take the time to housebreak your dog or solve whatever problem he has. See the appropriate entry in this chapter.

Barking indoors. Sometimes a sudden sound or noise will start a dog barking, as if a switch had been turned on in his brain. A ringing telephone with no one to answer it will certainly do so. Unplug the phone or hook it to an answering machine. Doorbells, door chimes, and door knockers used by strangers when you're not home very often start a chain of barking that could go on for ten or fifteen minutes. Try to arrange for deliveries when you're home or shift them to a neighbor's house.

Some dogs feel more secure in a dog crate when the family is away for a few hours. Depending on the dog, the crate can be left open and used as an indoor doghouse or have its wire door closed to confine the dog. A wire dog crate appeals to a dog's denning instincts. It looks like a cage, but to your dog it is a cave, the core area of his territory. In the wild a dog would take possession of a small cave, dig a large hole in the ground to hide in, or nestle in the hollow of a log. The dog crate is a sanctuary where he can get away from it all, making him feel secure to have a "den" where he can rest or sleep without worry. A large variety of dog crates are available in mail-order catalogs and at pet supply stores.

When you do not wish to use a dog crate, restrict a dog's access indoors with a puppy gate. See Puppygate in Chapter Five, "Shepherd Gear" (page 79). It is not recommended that a dog be shut away behind a closed door (a practice that can actually encourage barking). It not only creates a barking and whining problem but can negatively alter a dog's personality. With a puppy gate, the little dog sees out but remains confined in one room. The kitchen is the best place for this purpose. It is a fine alternative to a crate and less expensive.

Corrections when at home. Correct the dog every time he barks when you are home. Keep him attached to the leash and slip collar. If the doorbell rings, he will certainly bark. Use the corrective jerk to correct him. Also do so when he barks at noises or other dogs. Here, too, you may use a shake can or a water pistol in place of the leash and slip collar to correct the dog.

Permissible barking. It is quite possible that you may want your dog to bark at outside noises or strangers at your door. If you allowed the dog to bark in the past, you inadvertently encouraged him to do so. Now all you have to do is make some rules bringing into focus when he may or may not bark. Is it desirable for him to bark for ten seconds, thirty seconds, one minute, two minutes, or not at all? Correct him immediately if he is not allowed to bark at all, or allow a brief period of barking to pass before correcting him. Decide on how long he may bark and coordinate your corrections with that time frame. The same principle applies for what he is and is not allowed to bark at.

If you want your dog to learn to bark for a short period of time, do not use the word "NO!" with the correction. Use the word "CUT!" "No" means he did something wrong. "Cut" tells him to stop barking, that he did a good job. It is a very important distinction to the dog, and he will understand the difference if your tone of voice, body language, and attitude are firm but not harsh. Praise, immediately following the correction, is an important part of the reconditioning process. Allow the dog to bark for the desired time period, execute the corrective jerk while saying, "CUT," and then praise the dog for obeying.

Exercise. Exercise alone will not end your dog's barking problem but can certainly be a valuable part of the solution. Some dogs bark when left alone because they are bored, lonely, and sorely lacking a physical release for their energy. These conditions set the scene for canine mischief and destructiveness. Barking can be the least of the problems for such a dog.

An important answer, in part, is to exercise the dog before leaving him alone. A fifteen- to thirty-minute workout each morning before you leave the dog could eliminate much of his barking problem. A good daily regimen is a brisk morning walk for toileting purposes; a run; a "fetch" session with a ball, a stick, or a Frisbee; and then some playtime indoors. One good indoor game is "hide the biscuit." Show the dog the treat and place him behind a gate or in his crate so that he can see you hide the biscuit. Release him and say, "Go find!" Do it several times. If the weather prevents an outdoor workout, the morning is a perfect time to conduct obedience-training sessions. If the dog has already been trained, practice all his commands, developing them into a routine. Give him quick commands, three, four, or five times in a row. Mix them up so that he expends both mental and physical energy: "Heel . . . Sit . . . Heel . . . Sit . . . Heel . . . Sit," and so on.

The best thing you can do for your dog is work him out first thing in the morning instead of just a quick walk for toileting. It will tire him out and release his tension. An extra thirty minutes in the morning could make the difference between a good relationship with your neighbors and having to get rid of the dog.

Prevention Solutions

Have your dog walked by someone else. If you are away from home for eight to ten hours every day, you could hire someone to walk your dog. A midday walk could make a difference. It would help the dog dissipate his energy and relieve his frustration. If you cannot find a professional dog walker (they are listed in the Yellow Pages), perhaps you can hire someone in your neighborhood to perform the service. In large apartment houses a doorman will perform that service for a tip. Neighborhood kids are always looking for ways to earn after-school income. If the dog is friendly enough and the kid is responsible enough, you may never have to worry about excessive barking.

Confront all behavior problems. By solving all your dog's behavior problems, such as housebreaking and chewing, you may prevent a barking problem from developing.

Consult your neighbors. Ask around about whether your dog barks during the day. It is far better to get the bad news now, before the problem becomes severe.

Do not tie up the dog. Nothing leads to barking faster than frustrating a dog by tying him to a short tether or chain. If your dog must be confined, and many should be, use a wire dog crate or a puppy gate in the doorway of your kitchen.

Provide food and water. Be certain your dog is getting his full ration of food. If necessary, use an automatic feeder that works on a timer.

Provide shelter. Outdoor dogs must have some shelter, such as a doghouse or garage. There are special pet doors advertised in mail-order catalogs and dog magazines that allow the dog to enter your house or garage when the weather is bad.

Leave the blinds, shades, or curtains closed when you go out, so the dog has no opportunity to bark at people, animals, or moving objects.

Unplug the phone when you leave. Some dogs are driven to barking by an incessantly ringing telephone.

Place a DO NOT DISTURB sign on your door. A sign may prevent tradesmen from ringing the doorbell and setting off a long barking cycle. Have a DO NOT RING OR KNOCK. IT MAKES THE DOG BARK sign custom made.

Adjust the lights in your house. When you leave your dog, he may become mellow in subdued lighting or even darkness. The exact opposite may be true. Experiment.

Teach selectively. All dog owners should be aware that they often teach their dogs to behave in a particular manner without being aware of it. Pats on the head or verbal praise are accepted as rewards by the dog. They teach him to do whatever he did just before the "reward" was given. If you tell your dog he is a good boy immediately after he barked, you have, in effect, taught him to bark. This can be useful or counterproductive, depending on your needs (see Permissible Barking, page 150).

Make a chart. For one week, note the time of day or night whenever your dog barks and what makes him bark. This will be the most useful aid in preventing excessive barking. The chart will help you develop the overview of the dog's behavior. Look at the chart to decide what is desirable for the dog to bark at and what isn't. With this knowledge, you know when to correct the dog. Use the chart in conjunction with the techniques in Permissible Barking.

Chewing

Of all the behavior problems of dogs, destructive chewing is the most upsetting, even more so than housebreaking mistakes. A mess on the carpet can be cleaned up. But when the arm is chewed off a leather couch, your only options are to live with it or buy another one. Not only is chewing behavior exasperating, it is expensive and at times very upsetting. When a dog chews up a stamp collection or an antique, he has probably destroyed years of effort and expense. Many a new dog owner has lost a personal treasure to the teeth of dogs that chewed up the home. A dog with a chewing problem will damage furniture, curtains, appliances, books, shoes, clothing, and anything else available for him to sink his teeth into, including doors, walls, and baseboards. Some dog owners have lost hundreds and sometimes thousands of dollars in personal possessions. A canine chewer does not win the hearts and minds of his family. This unhappiness and disappointment can be avoided with a little knowledge and effort. Chewing problems are not difficult to solve.

Creating an aversion to chewing your possessions is the most effective way to stop this behavior. It's easy. Simply make your stuff taste awful. The best way to do this is to mix a thick paste consisting of alum powder and water. (Alum powder can be bought over the counter at any drugstore and is inexpensive.) Mix the powder with a small amount of water until it is the consistency of mustard. Smear the mixture on the dog's favorite chewing items. The alum paste does not stain and washes off easily. It tastes unpleasantly bitter and has a contracting, puckering effect on a dog's tongue and mouth. It makes

Most chewing problems start in puppyhood, when they are easily corrected.

destructive chewing an unappealing experience. Although alum is not harmful if eaten, it should be used in small quantities. The mixture could upset a dog if swallowed in large quantities. Given its unpleasant taste, it is unlikely that a dog will lick very much of it.

Do not confine your pet improperly. Some dogs will chew anything and everything in an attempt to escape or relieve their emotional stress if they are confined in a room behind a closed door. Most will whimper, bark, and eventually chew on whatever they can find. If a dog is left alone behind a closed door, his chewing behavior may become frantic and destructive.

An untrained dog with or without a chewing problem should *not* have the run of the house when left alone. He should be confined properly. See Puppygate, page 79.

Most chewing problems start in puppyhood, when they are easily prevented from becoming serious. If your puppy starts to chew on any of your possessions, discourage him immediately by saying,

"NO," in a firm tone of voice. Praise the dog immediately afterward and give him a chew toy made of nylon or rawhide to gnaw on. This redirects the chewing behavior away from your possessions. Do not allow your puppy to chew on anything that remotely resembles furniture, clothing, carpeting, curtains, or things you value. Never give your dog an old shoe or a knotted towel to chew on, because sooner or later he will look for the good stuff. Avoid dog toys such as a latex pork chop or a rolled newspaper. Give him a nylon or rawhide chew toy or a large, hard ball that he can call his own.

The chewing behavior of puppies is almost always caused by teething. This will continue for the first six months of his life. Soak several washcloths in cold water, squeeze them, stretch them into rope shape, and freeze them. When they are cold and hard, give them to your dog to chew on, one at a time. Each one will stay cold for at least sixty minutes. As he chews on them, the coldness will numb his gums and ease his pain.

Some dogs chew because of the emotional stress they experience when left alone or because they are bored or because chewing has become a habit ignored in a puppy. It is a popular misconception that dogs chew destructively for spite or to punish their owners for leaving them alone. This is incorrect. Spite and revenge are based on human feelings and thoughts.

Never punish a dog with a chewing problem. It is counterproductive and changes nothing except to add to his emotional stress. If you understand what makes your dog chew, you are more likely to correct the problem by changing the conditions that have caused it. Play a radio softly in the background when he is alone. Give him many chew toys with which to distract himself.

If all else fails, you can give your dog a correction, but only if you actually catch him in the act of chewing. A verbal correction, "NO," is usually effective. A particularly stubborn dog may require a leash correction. Read the entire first portion of Chapter Eight, "Obedience-Training Your German Shepherd."

Digging

All dogs will dig up your yard or front lawn if you give them the opportunity. German Shepherds love to dig and roll in the soft ground. Consequently, Shepherd puppies should be supervised when allowed outdoors. If they attempt to dig, say, "NO," in a very firm tone of voice. Your young dog will be somewhat startled, causing him to stop. Praise him immediately for stopping. This is very important. Do not leave your puppy outside, unattended, on a soft surface. Put him in an exercise pen sitting on concrete or on grass with chicken wire spread over the bottom.

The correct use of chicken wire is one of the best self-correcting methods available. Most dogs are drawn to the same holes they dug before, even if they are filled in with the original dirt. Fill your dog's favorite hole with a layer of chicken wire close to the surface and cover it with dirt. This makes it unpleasant for digging. You can also fill in the existing holes with large rocks. They are unpleasant for the dog to dig his paws into and discourage him from digging further.

Chicken wire is not only the best filler, it is also the best deterrent when used to cover the ground the dog likes to dig in. Use it in three- to six-foot lengths and cover it with a thin coating of dirt. If your dog moves his digging activities to another location, cover that with chicken wire, too. Do not let him see you laying the wire or he will dig in another location and fail to undergo the self-teaching experience. The idea is to make digging as difficult and disagreeable as possible. If you correct the problem in puppyhood, you will avoid serious consequences when the dog is fully grown.

Jumping on People

German Shepherd puppies are cute when they greet you with enthusiasm and jump all over you in an attempt to lick your face. As they get older—and larger—they must place their front paws on your chest to balance themselves as they attempt to say hello. They will jump all over you to let you know how glad they are to see you, just like any other dog does. But as fully grown dogs, they are very large and strong. They can easily knock you down or bruise your body without meaning any harm. Their uncontrolled energy and enthusiasm will gladden the heart and hurt your body. This behavior is also annoying and inconvenient when you are dressed up for a social or business engagement. A full-grown Shepherd that jumps on you will smudge your clothes with whatever is on his paws and wrinkle your freshly pressed outfit. If you are wearing makeup, he will smear it as he slurps your face.

Even obedience-trained dogs jump up on people if they are not consistently corrected every time they do it. Some Shepherds will jump on anyone they like, whether they are out on the street or at home. They like to jump on people as an expression of pleasure. This is also how they tell you they want to play, eat, or get your attention.

Sooner or later even the nicest dog that is allowed to jump on people will create an unpleasant situation. While many people enjoy a dog's attention, many are frightened when a dog jumps on them, especially children. Being jumped on by a dog makes some people angry. You cannot expect a dog to know the difference between who likes it and who doesn't. The no-jumping rule should apply at all times and in every situation. Either the dog is allowed to jump on everyone or he is allowed to jump on no one. There can be no in-between here without confusing the dog and frustrating the family.

When the various members of the family are inconsistent about the dog's jumping, it encourages this behavior to continue, especially when it is inappropriate and inconvenient. Do not allow the dog to jump up on you when you feel playful and then forbid it when you are not up for it. This is confusing and unfair. You can stop your dog from jumping only if you are diligent about correcting him *every time* he jumps on someone, including yourself. Before attempting to deal with this behavior, you must ask yourself if you want your dog to stop jumping on people. If the answer is yes, please continue.

Teaching your dog *not* to jump on people is easy. It simply requires a correction whenever he jumps. If applied properly, a leash correction (the corrective jerk) solves the problem. Read the entire first portion of Chapter Eight, "Obedience-Training Your German Shepherd," with particular attention to The Corrective Jerk.

The leash correction is best for correcting jumping behavior. Dogs usually jump on their owners when they come home, or when seeing people they like. Place the leash and training collar on your dog and set up a similar situation in which another member of the household walks through the door and you are prepared to grab the leash and make the correction. When the dog jumps on the person coming through the door, jerk the leash firmly to the right, and at the same time say, "NO," in a firm tone of voice. The firmness of the jerk and the force of your voice must be appropriate for the age and temperament of your dog. Obviously, a puppy or sensitive dog must be handled with less vigor than a typical adult dog. Stubborn dogs should be corrected with the shake can technique described below.

Praise the dog immediately for responding to the correction (even if his response was not perfect). Praise immediately following a correction is of vital importance. The dog will probably jump up again if you make yourself available. (Do not invite him to jump on you, though.) The instant he does, give him another leash correction accompanied by a firm "NO." Always use the firm "NO" as part of any correction so that eventually the verbal correction alone will suffice. Correct the dog each time he jumps on you or on anyone else and he will eventually change his ways.

Stubborn dogs that do not respond properly to a leash correction require a noise correction with the use of a simple, improvised training tool called the shake can. Take an empty soda can, wash it, and slip ten pennies into it. Tape the opening so the pennies cannot fall out. Now shake the can vigorously. It will make a very commanding rattle similar to the sound of a New Year's Eve noisemaker. This is an ideal way to correct an obstinate dog. It easily gets his attention when shaken loudly and accompanied by a very firm "NO!" It also enables you to deliver a correction anytime and anyplace because it does not require a leash and training collar.

For a number of reasons it is important to hold the shake can behind your back when you use it. The rattling sound can be too startling

even for a stubborn dog or puppy. Making a dog fearful is very unkind and not the basis for a good relationship. Creating fear should
never be a part of dog training or problem solving. Also, by shaking
the can behind your back, you will avoid creating fearful associations
with your hand movements or gestures. The rattling sound simply
serves to get the dog's attention and as a background noise to your
loud, firm "NO!" The most important aspect of any correction is the
word "NO" sharply delivered in a firm tone of voice. Eventually,
the dog will always respond properly to a simple "NO" from you or
the members of your family.

For very sensitive dogs and puppies, use a small squirt bottle of
water as a corrective tool rather than the leash and collar or shake
can. The squirt bottle should be the kind used to spray house plants.
Hold it behind your back. When the dog jumps on you, spray him
gently in the face with one quick sprinkle of water. As you do, say,
"NO," in a firm tone of voice. Do not forget to praise the dog immediately after. The squirt bottle is effective yet gentle.

To avoid the problem entirely, do not allow your puppy to jump
on you, even though he is cute and adorable. If you correct him when
he tries it, he will never do it as an adult dog.

Assuming the dog has been obedience-trained, he should be commanded to "SIT" immediately following any correction. Praise the
dog after he obeys the command. If he has *not* been obedience-trained,
the corrective jerk is all you can use until the dog is brought under
control through training. He may still try to jump after the first jerk.
Correct the dog every time he jumps until he stops.

Dogs that jump on people almost always indulge this upsetting
behavior while outside for a walk. When it happens, the tendency for
dog owners is to pull the dog away. Instead, give him a corrective
jerk, a firm "NO," and enthusiastic praise for jumping down. Immediately turn and swiftly walk in the opposite direction. Perform this
sequence every time the dog jumps on someone while out for a walk
and the problem will end.

Bear in mind that the problem will continue forever if you, your
family, your friends, or neighbors allow the dog to jump on them at

any time. Make it clear to everyone that he must never be invited to jump on them or be encouraged by petting him or giving him any form of approval for this unwanted behavior.

A word of caution. Do not knock your dog off you with a hard knee to his chest in order to stop him from jumping. Do not step on his toes for this or any other reason. Do not use force of any kind to push the dog off you. These gestures are not only painful, they are medically dangerous.

Using training techniques that hurt your dog destroys the chances of having a happy, satisfying relationship with him. They could make your dog aggressive with strangers and shy with you. No right-thinking person uses pain to teach a child anything, so why would anyone do that to a loving, trusting dog? Training techniques based on pain are ineffective and harmful to the dog's personality. To solve the problem of jumping on people, be consistent in your use of the correction techniques offered here as they are needed.

Mouthing and Nipping

Mouthing. This seemingly harmless activity is usually not recognized as a behavior problem and, as a matter of fact, is often thought of as cute. However, when a puppy (or adult dog) mouths, he puts his open mouth on your hand, your arm, your leg, or anything that belongs to you, including any and all of your possessions. This behavior quickly loses its charms as your clothing begins to soak with your dog's saliva and your possessions become seriously damaged from the saturation and the teeth marks. The worst result of mouthing is its progression into a nipping and biting problem.

Nipping. Everyone smiles when puppies take fingers into their mouths and nibble on them like Ritz crackers. No one seems to realize that this is a sneak preview of biting problems. A nip from a puppy usually involves the front teeth and feels like a slight pinch without full pressure. The nip may or may not be painful, but that is not the point. Unfortunately, nipping is not considered to be a behavior problem by dog owners until the nipper turns into a biter.

Mouthing and nipping problems can be attributed to the oral inclinations of the breed, to teething pain, and to the wrong kind of stimulation from the dog's family.

As with human babies, teething is characterized by soreness and itching of the gums, along with some slight bleeding and drooling. When puppies and young dogs teethe, all their energy and concentration become focused on relieving the discomfort of their gums by chewing, nipping, and mouthing. If allowed to go uncorrected, this behavior becomes generalized and habitual.

Owner-induced behavior is often the cause of nipping and mouthing. Playing aggressive games such as tug-of-war with an old sock or tennis shoe in a puppy's teeth, with seemingly humorous pulling and growling, encourages mouthing, nipping, and, eventually, biting. Boxing and wrestling with your dog has the same effect. Placing your fingers in the dog's mouth as a form of amusement also creates these problems. Hitting your dog can induce him to fight back with his teeth. Pushing him away with your hands can inspire your puppy to nip at you. When you are grooming your dog or giving him medicine, he will nip or mouth if you hurt him. If what you do with your hands causes your dog pain, he will nip and mouth you until it becomes a more serious behavior problem. A puppy should never be allowed to use his teeth on any human being for any reason.

Mouthing and Nipping Solutions

Teething. When mouthing and nipping are caused by teething, the solution is to alleviate the dog's pain and discomfort. Soak several washcloths in cold water. Twist them and put them in the freezer. Once they are frozen, give them to the puppy one at a time as chew toys. Each frozen washcloth will stay cold for at least sixty minutes. The coldness will numb the dog's gums and ease his pain. Another possibility is to freeze an entire bowl of water and allow the dog to lick it all day long. Chew toys are also beneficial. Use hard rubber toys, rawhide bones, and synthetic bones made of hard, digestible nylon.

Corrections. Correcting your dog when you catch him nipping or mouthing is the most effective method of stopping this unwanted behavior and preventing it from becoming permanent. There are three types of acceptable corrections: verbal corrections, shake-can corrections, and leash corrections.

Verbal corrections: Reprimand the dog by saying, "NO," in a firm tone of voice. This will be effective for most puppies and dogs. Following the correction, praise your dog lavishly and redirect his desire to chew with a substitute chew toy.

Shake-can corrections: This is an alternative for dogs that do not respond to your verbal corrections. The shake can is a homemade training tool that works when your dog is not wearing a leash and collar. Take several empty soda cans, wash them, and slip ten pennies into each one. Tape the opening so the pennies cannot fall out. When you shake the can vigorously it will make a loud, commanding rattle. It is meant to get your dog's attention and give him a negative message.

Place the shake cans in the areas where your dog is likely to nip or mouth. When he misbehaves, shake the can behind your back and say, "NO," in a firm tone of voice. After each correction, praise him lavishly and give him a substitute chew toy.

Leash corrections: See The Corrective Jerk in Chapter Eight, "Obedience-Training Your German Shepherd" (page 114). Leash corrections are an important training tool when all else fails. Of all the corrections, this one is the most effective for dogs that do not respond to anything else.

Correct the dog with a quick little jerk of the leash, but only when he is actually nipping or mouthing.

After each correction, praise your dog and give him a chew toy or nylon bone as a substitution for your hand.

CHAPTER TEN

Keeping Your German Shepherd Dog Healthy

Devoted dog owners can give their pets a happy, vigorous life with preventive medicine, healthy care, and common sense. When you are living with a young Good Shepherd, it is hard to envision the possibility of your dog being sick. Nevertheless, it is unrealistic to avoid the subject. In the war against sickness, information is the most powerful weapon; a veterinarian is your greatest ally; and the concept of preventive medicine, the most effective strategy.

Vaccinations

Vaccinations are the foundation of modern preventive medicine. When it comes to saving the lives of dogs, antiviral and antibacterial vaccines are the most significant weapons available against disease. Millions of dogs have been spared the effects of debilitating sickness and painful death because of the immunities provided by vaccinations.

Vaccines are preparations of *killed* or *modified live* (weakened) strains of disease-causing agents that are injected into the body. They stimulate the immune system and promote the formation of antibodies, which attack and kill specific viruses or bacteria. It is like fighting fire with fire. Vaccines are intended to create immunity to the specific diseases they introduce into the body. Please note: A very small number of vaccinated animals do not get full immunity from every vaccine. Most vaccinated dogs, however, achieve full immunity and avoid the diseases for which they have been immunized.

When a puppy is first born, it receives *colostrum* with the first feedings of mother's milk. Colostrum creates a population of antibodies in the newborn puppy that fight disease for the first four to six weeks of life. This protection, however, is temporary, and while active in the body, it interferes with the effectiveness of most vaccines that may be introduced. Consequently, puppies are not vaccinated until they are weaned from mother's milk at approximately six weeks of age. The vaccine for kennel cough *(Bordetella bronchiseptica)* is an exception; puppies as young as two weeks of age may be vaccinated for this infection.

Depending upon the veterinarian's point of view, the breeder, and the nature of the vaccines used, puppies may be vaccinated at six, eight, twelve, sixteen, or perhaps twenty weeks of age. They are usually vaccinated with a combination of vaccines that must be repeated every year. Puppies and dogs can be vaccinated for canine distemper, infectious canine hepatitis, rabies, canine parvovirus, and kennel cough in combination with vaccines for leptospirosis, canine coronavirus, and Lyme disease *(Lyme borreliosis)*. All dogs must be given annual "booster shots" (yearly vaccinations) for the rest of their life if they are to maintain immunity.

The Annual Checkup

Many medical problems are prevented, or at least caught early, at a dog's annual medical examination. It is essential for pet owners to understand the importance of a complete annual checkup for their dogs. A typical veterinary examination should include looking at both ears, the nose, mouth, teeth, throat, respiratory system, spine or musculoskeletal system, skin, legs, abdominal cavity, cardiovascular system, anal area, and genitalia. An annual checkup is the time to have your dog vaccinated for the first time or revaccinated with booster shots. If your dog is sick or if the veterinarian suspects a possible medical problem, she or he may ask for one or more laboratory tests involving stool samples, blood tests, or X-rays.

Exercise

Exercise is an important means of preventing sickness and promoting good health. German Shepherds that work as protection dogs or guard dogs and remain outdoors much of the time have an excellent opportunity to stay in good physical and mental condition. The exercise from their work and their having a useful function is very beneficial to their well-being. Dogs living as pets, however, must be exercised and allowed to express their energetic exuberance, or they become vulnerable to medical problems associated with lethargy and boredom. Exercise for dogs can simply be a few games, a walk, a run, a swim, or anything that involves exertion. Maintaining good muscle tone is important, but most of all, exercising a German Shepherd should be fun. It also strengthens the loving bond between the dog and his family.

In general terms, a dog's need for exercise should be based on the physical activity for which its breed was created. Specifically, a German Shepherd is a strong, muscular, and energetic dog born to do all that is necessary to protect and maintain its territory and those who are part of it. German Shepherds are large, vigorous dogs with a great need to use their strength, agility, and energy. Exercise is important not only for the body but for dogs' mental stability and happiness as well. Shepherds without a daily opportunity for physical exertion go through life unfulfilled. While it is not necessary for Good Shepherds living as pets to be sentry dogs, they must have energy-consuming activities *with their family* that give them a sense of pleasure and purpose.

Dogs that are exercised as puppies develop better than those that aren't. Most dogs are considered middle-aged at seven years because that is when their metabolic system begins to slow down. The food they consume converts more readily to fat unless it is burned off in

Canine sports, such as agility tournaments, are ideal sources of exercise for German Shepherd Dogs.

some form of physical activity. German Shepherds, especially those living in cities, should be given two or more walks a day, a good run (depending on their age), and some vigorous playtime.

A puppy needs only ten or twenty minutes of exercise several times a day. The best exercise for puppies is free play with another dog or several toys and a human. Even at the earliest age, games involving chasing a ball or some other tossed toy are best. It is hard to overdo it with a puppy because they all stop playing when they get tired and know when to rest. Many activities designed for dogs are ideal sources of exercise, including just about all the organized canine sports and activities (dog shows, field trials, obedience trials, and dog agility tournaments). Training your German Shepherd Dog for simple obedience is a wonderful way to provide exercise.

A young dog should get at least thirty minutes of walking, running, playing, or jogging once or twice a day. *Do not jog with a puppy. Do not run dogs of any age by your side while on a bicycle, with or without a leash attached*. A dog must never be dragged by the leash or put in danger of getting in front of the wheels of any moving vehicle.

Middle-aged and older dogs must also be exercised, but with more moderation and caution than with younger dogs. Gentle walks, carefully thrown balls, and games of your own invention are best.

Never exercise a dog immediately after he has eaten. Large dogs, such as German Shepherds, are vulnerable to the life-threatening medical condition commonly known as *bloat*, which can be brought about by strenuous activity immediately following a meal. See Gastric Dilation-Volvulus *(bloat)* in Chapter Twelve, "Medical Problems Common to German Shepherd Dog" (page 194).

Take your puppy or adult dog for walks on a regular basis as often as possible, even if it's only for an errand. An occasional weekend of exercise is worse than none at all because it can strain the body, especially on an older dog. Consistency is the most important and beneficial aspect of exercise. Giving your adult dog a long, hard run once a day or several times a week is also beneficial.

Playing fetch with a flying disc (Frisbee) will please any dog, including a German Shepherd. You can get the same enjoyable effect, though, from a large ball or a stick. Use almost anything that promotes a run-and-fetch game. However, do not use a tennis ball, because it can lodge in the throat or be chewed into pieces, both of which have obvious consequences.

Grooming and Hygiene

Essential elements of good health are hygiene and grooming. These go far to prevent sickness and disease. This section does not cover the intricacies of dog grooming for its own sake. Entire books exist for that purpose, and dog-grooming salons are available everywhere for the dog owner desiring that service. In this section grooming as it applies to hygiene is the concern. A limited grooming effort is necessary to maintain good health for all German Shepherd Dogs. For the necessary equipment, see Grooming Tools in Chapter Five, "Shepherd Gear" (page 85).

The German Shepherd coat. Like many dog breeds, the Good Shepherd is "double-coated," which means it is covered with an outer coat and an undercoat. The outer coat is the most visible and defines the look of the dog in terms of color and coat pattern. It lies flat and close to the body, consists of straight hair with no waves, and is of medium length. The outer coat is also dense, hard-textured, and water resistant. The undercoat is abundantly thick, woolly, and softer than the outercoat. The hair on the head, legs, and paws is considerably shorter than on the dog's trunk. There is usually a thick ruff of longer hair around the neck (when the dog is in full coat) that tends to stand away from the skin.

Brushing and combing. Shepherds are expected to have a natural look with no clipping of the coat at all. However, they should be brushed at least twice a week (or more) to maintain cleanliness and luster. A bristle brush and slicker brush are each used for brushing, but for different purposes. See Brushes in Chapter Five, "Shepherd Gear" (page 85), for more information. Brushing and then combing keeps the coat clean and stimulates the skin. These important weekly grooming procedures are as much for the sake of good hygiene as they are for good looks. It is an opportunity to place loving hands on your pet as you check for tumors, abrasions, injuries, fleas, ticks, and other signs of poor health.

Baths. Shepherds do not require baths unless they are unusually dirty or odorous. Bathing your pet twice a year is sufficient unless the dog is going to be shown or entered into one of the competitive dog sports. Frequent brushing and combing avoids the need for repeated baths.

Nails. A German Shepherd's nails should be clipped when they are no longer even with the surface of the paw pad. Neglected nails, if not worn down naturally from hard surfaces, can throw a dog off balance and irritate the paw. Use a guillotine-type nail trimmer, holding it vertically while holding the dog's paw up to it. Insert the protruding nail into the circular opening. Trim away a small amount of nail at a time until you are confident enough to snip off the nail in one slice. Do not trim too close to the *quick,* which is a thin, red-to-pink

A German Shepherd's coat should be brushed at least twice a week.

vein, or the nail will bleed. A good rule to follow is to cut at the point where the nails begin to curve. If the nail should bleed, apply an antiseptic coagulant powder or styptic pencil, which can be purchased at any drugstore or pet supply store.

Ears. Ears should be kept clean and free of wax deposits with a cloth wrapped around your finger or with a cotton swab dipped in baby oil or peroxide. Do not penetrate too deeply into the canal, to avoid causing an injury. If it makes you nervous to clean your Shepherd's ears, have a professional groomer or veterinarian take care of this important aspect of hygiene.

Teeth. Oral hygiene is as important to pets as it is to humans and should not be overlooked. It is desirable to clean your dog's teeth at least once a week to avoid extensive veterinary dental treatment. Most pets require sedation or anesthesia for thorough dental cleaning and therapy.

Canine toothbrushes and cleaning agents designed specifically for dogs are readily available in most pet supply stores and catalogs. Baking soda mixed into a paste with water is quite effective and can substitute for any commercially manufactured canine toothpaste. You may use a clean washcloth to scrub your dog's teeth, provided there is little hardened plaque accumulated on their surface. *Under no circumstances should toothpaste meant for humans be used on a dog. It can be harmful.* Ask your veterinarian about regular care of your dog's teeth.

Canine Medical Conditions

Keeping your dog in good health requires an understanding of when he is in bad health. It is essential for dog owners to have some basis for knowing when something is wrong. This uncomplicated information is important to have. It can be of great value when the question of taking your dog to a veterinarian arises.

It is not difficult to know when your dog is sick if you know what is normal and what is abnormal for him. Annual checkups help a great deal, but knowing your dog's normal physical condition, behavior, and body language is of greater help. When your dog is sick, he requires medical attention. Knowing when to take your dog to a veterinarian could save his life.

Signs and Symptoms of Canine Sickness

Limping
Loss of balance
Paralysis
Difficulty moving the neck or back
Difficulty changing body position
Listlessness, lethargy, passivity
Loss of appetite
Unusual increase in appetite
Excessive weight gain or loss
Fever (normal range is 100°F to 102.5°F)
Vomiting
Prolonged diarrhea

Excessive thirst
Prolonged lack of thirst
Head shaking
Swiping ears with paws
Increased urination
Inability to urinate
Painful urination
Discolored urine (pink, red, dark yellow, or orange)
Loss of urinary control, especially in sleeping area
Coughing
Troublesome, labored, or inconsistent breathing
Pale or discolored gums
Abnormal scratching
Hair loss
Changes of skin tone (redness, sores, lumps, openings, crusts,
    scales, discharges, or changes of color)
Seizures
Bleeding
Inflammation of the eyes
Excessive tearing
Excessive sneezing
Constant nasal discharge
Mouth odor
Inability to chew
Whimpering

Serious Canine Infectious Diseases

Although *The Good Shepherd* is not a medical manual, it would be a serious omission and a disservice to fail to provide information about the medical conditions included here. The following diseases are very serious and, in many cases, life-threatening. They cannot be diagnosed or treated by anyone other than a veterinarian. Nevertheless, recognizing the early signs of disease and getting prompt veterinary attention can be of significant value. The information is presented here to help dog owners understand the seriousness of these diseases so that they can give their dogs the best chance for survival.

Canine Distemper

This highly contagious disease is caused by a virus similar to the one that causes measles in humans. Reports indicate that canine distemper, worldwide, is the leading cause of death from infectious disease in dogs. It is seen most commonly in puppies between three and eight months of age, especially if they have not been vaccinated. At this age young dogs are weaned and can no longer benefit from the protection provided by colostrum, which creates a population of natural antibodies and is present in mothers' milk.

Signs. Canine distemper affects several areas of the body, including the respiratory system, the intestines, the skin, and the brain. Secondary infections are common and can result in death. The first sign of distemper appears approximately three to fifteen days after exposure. Because the early signs are very subtle, symptoms may not be apparent for two to three weeks.

Stage 1: The signs are similar to those of human upper respiratory infections, including high fever, loss of appetite, and watery discharge from the eyes and nose. This can be accompanied by a dry, hacking cough. Diarrhea may also be present, leading to dehydration. Secondary infections such as skin lesions or even pneumonia may develop.

Stage 2: Brain involvement may be seen after two to three weeks of infection. Periods of head shaking, chewing motions, and slobbering may be observed. Epileptic-like seizures may occur. The infected dog may also move uncontrollably in circles as it kicks and yelps. These symptoms are followed by confusion and aimless walking, with no recognition of anyone familiar. The prognosis for dogs with brain involvement is usually death.

A secondary bacterial infection that sometimes results from distemper is called "hard pad"; it attacks the skin of the feet and nose. The pads form thick calous-like growths, and the nose becomes thickened and horn-like. When this condition develops, there usually are accompanying signs of encephalitis.

Treatment. Prevention is the only real help. Immunization early in a puppy's life plus annual booster shots offers the best hope. Antibiotics are not effective against canine distemper but are given to support the secondary involvement of bacterial infections. Intravenous fluids are given to prevent dehydration. Anticonvulsants and sedatives are administered to control seizures. Medication is given to control diarrhea. The success of your veterinarian's treatment depends on the speed with which the dog receives professional care and the strength of the dog to fight off the virus.

Infectious Canine Hepatitis

Infectious canine hepatitis is a viral disease that is highly contagious and transmitted only to dogs. It affects the liver, the lining of the blood vessels, and the kidneys. It is a major cause of death in puppies and young dogs that are not vaccinated. The virus is passed from all body secretions of carrier dogs and is present in the urine of dogs several months after recovery. Dogs of all ages are susceptible. Infection is caused by ingesting contaminated material.

Signs. Canine hepatitis has a wide range of symptoms that can vary from mild at the beginning to furious episodes leading ultimately to death. In some cases the signs of hepatitis are confused with canine distemper. The first sign is fever, often above 104°F, which may subside after twenty-four to forty-eight hours. Occasionally, a fever that lasts only one or two days is the sole sign of the disease, although blood tests reveal a low leukocyte count. In some cases the fever lasts longer than three or four days. Other signs include increased thirst, lack of appetite, depression, and excessive watering of the eyes and nose. Diarrhea, vomiting, spasms, and heavy and rapid breathing are also signs of this painful disease.

Puppies are very susceptible in the first few months of life, although dogs of any age can contract the virus. Shortly after exposure the virus is secreted in the urine, saliva, and stool. It is in this stage that the dog is most contagious. Even dogs that are recuperating can shed the virus for months afterward. In the extreme, fatal form, puppies can die without obvious illness. Some infected dogs become ill suddenly with bloody diarrhea, collapse, and die. In the acute form, the dog suffers from aggravated diarrhea, loss of appetite, and high fever. Other symptoms of the disease are photophobia (sensitivity to light), jaundice (yellowing of the eyes), and swelling of the liver characterized by a tucked-up appearance of the belly and accompanied by painful movements. In its mildest form, the dog may only show loss of appetite, be lethargic, or just appear to be having a bad day. **Treatment.** Blood tests can determine the diagnosis. If the disease is uncomplicated, it will run its course within one week with professional care. In such a case the dog will probably remain in the hospital or with the veterinarian for at least seven days. There is no therapy, however, for the disease itself. Treatment can only minimize the effects of shock and hemorrhaging, and prevent secondary bacterial infection. The attending vet may introduce intravenous fluid therapy, blood transfusions, and antibiotics as well as corticosteroids. The only defense against infectious canine hepatitis is early vaccination and annual boosters, which are important because there is no permanent immunity.

Rabies

Rabies is a fatal disease threatening all warm-blooded animals. In most industrialized countries throughout the world, cases of rabies involving humans have been eliminated almost entirely as a result of effective vaccination programs aimed at domestic dogs and cats. Incidents of rabies infecting dogs and cats are reported in relatively low numbers, but nevertheless serve as a frightening reminder that this deadly disease is far from being eradicated. In the United States animals transmitting the disease are primarily skunks, raccoons, wild foxes, bats, and woodchucks (the only rodents involved to any great extent).

The rabies virus is spread through contact with saliva from an infected animal, usually transmitted through a bite. Saliva can also transmit the disease if it comes in direct contact with an open wound or through mucous membrane tissue (the lining of internal surfaces of the body, such as the mouth, digestive tract, respiratory tract, and urinary tract).

Incubation averages between three and eight weeks, but there have been cases with incubation as short as one week or as long as one year. The virus is carried quickly to the central nervous system. It reaches the spinal cord within four to five days and travels upward until it ultimately infects the brain. During this period it also travels to the salivary gland and can then be transmitted to another animal when bitten.

Signs. Rabies has two stages, the "furious" and the "dumb." The furious form lasts approximately one week and is identified by behavioral changes, including restlessness and characteristics contrary to the dog's personality, such as irritability, high energy in a normally sedate dog, or lethargy in a normally energetic dog. Friendly dogs become aggressive and shy. Shy dogs may become overly affectionate. Eventually the dog will avoid people, become aloof, and often stare off into space. A dog in the furious stage may also become ferocious and bite any person or animal that comes close.

Fever, nausea, and diarrhea are common. Dogs in this stage are sensitive to light and to being touched. Eventually they will chew violently on any restraint, such as a leash, or on the metal parts of their wire crate. In this condition the rabid dog, drooling, panting, frothing at the mouth as a result of rapid breathing through the saliva, may die from a convulsive seizure without progressing to the final, "dumb" stage, which takes the form of partial or total paralysis.

The dumb stage continues with diminishing aspects of the furious form as the head and neck muscles become paralyzed. The dog suffers. Mercifully, death ensues within one or two days.

Treatment. Rabies represents a fatal disease for dogs and humans, once the signs and symptoms become evident. It is highly dangerous to attempt treatment of rabid dogs because of the great risk of infection to health caregivers.

Humans can be treated *before* clinical signs appear. For this reason, *immediate* medical attention is required following a bite from an animal suspected of rabies. Once the symptoms become evident, the disease is usually fatal in dogs and humans alike.

All dog owners are advised to have their pets vaccinated for rabies at three months of age and again twelve months later. The dog should then be revaccinated every three years or as instructed by the manufacturers of the vaccine.

Parvovirus

"Parvo" is a highly contagious virus that is transmitted to the body orally by contact with infected feces and possibly through urine droplets. It can be carried on the bottom of shoes or transported on any other object. Dogs of any age can be affected, although puppies under the age of five months have the highest mortality rate. Elderly dogs are also more susceptible. This deadly disease is seen in two forms:

Parvoviral enteritis. This form enters the body through the oral cavity; it attacks the tonsils first and then is concentrated within the entire intestinal tract, impairing all normal functions of digestion and resulting in life-threatening loss of fluids and body weight.

Signs. The enteritis form causes unrelenting bloody diarrhea, painful vomiting, depression, and dehydration. Infected puppies will run high temperatures, and older dogs will run unusually low temperatures. Other signs are severe coughing and swelling of the cornea of the eye. The onset of parvo is sudden and bewildering, and without immediate veterinary treatment the dog dies in a matter of days.

The incubation period is approximately seven to fourteen days after exposure. The first signs are severe depression and loss of appetite.

A second form of this deadly disease is parvoviral myocarditis.

Parvoviral myocarditis. This form is seen almost exclusively in puppies under three months of age. Myocarditis is an inflammation of the heart muscle that leads to heart failure and death and occurs in pups from nonimmune mothers. Puppies affected will stop nursing and develop difficulty breathing. Death usually occurs suddenly between the ages of three and eight weeks. This form of parvo has become rare because of routine vaccination of most dogs.

Treatment. There is no antiviral therapy for canine parvovirus available. Survival and treatment depend on the form of parvo contracted, the age of the dog, the severity of the infection, and the speed with which the dog receives professional care. Prompt action by the pet owner is often a life-and-death factor.

The veterinarian's objective is to stabilize the dog until the body's immune system clears the infection. Massive fluid loss through diarrhea and vomiting is the principal cause of death. Therefore, replacement of body fluids plays a major role in recovery. Intravenous (IV) fluids and medications (administered through a vein) are essential in replacing fluid loss and controlling vomiting and diarrhea. Broad-spectrum antibiotics are given to prevent or fight secondary bacterial infections, such as pneumonia. Hospitalization is necessary.

Prevention begins with vaccination of the mother before pregnancy with modified live vaccine. Annual booster shots are necessary. If the puppies are vaccinated at too early an age, the antibodies from mother's milk will not only cause vaccine failure but will prevent them from developing their own active immune response. The first few months of life offer ample opportunity for parvovirus to develop.

If a dog or puppy becomes infected with parvovirus, separate it from other dogs in the household or kennel and minimize contact between sick and healthy animals. Clean all of the dog's areas with hot, soapy water to remove possibly infected litter and then disinfect with a 1:32 dilution of chlorine bleach and water to kill the persistent virus, which is not easily eradicated.

Canine Infectious Tracheobronchitis ("Kennel Cough")

This inflammation of the upper throat, trachea, and bronchi is a persistent illness that is viewed as a complex clinical syndrome produced by various infectious bacteria and viruses, at times in combination. Among them are:

Bordetella bronchiseptica, the most dominant infecting agent of the kennel cough complex. It is a bacterium that is capable of causing severe tracheobronchitis on its own without the invasion of other pathogens in the syndrome;

Canine parainfluenza virus, another element in the kennel cough complex. It is a virus belonging to the same family as canine distemper viruses and produces a mild to moderately severe infection in the windpipe and large air passages of the lungs;

Canine adenovirus-2, a DNA-containing virus that causes upper respiratory tract infections;

Mycoplasmas, microorganisms that are bacteria-like, inhabiting the respiratory and genital tracts of dogs. Parasitic in nature, they exist without cell walls and require no oxygen. They are considered to be a contributing factor to the kennel cough syndrome in some cases. They are capable of initiating upper respiratory disease on their own in some rare instances;

Canine distemper virus, although a more severe disease producing intense systemic illness, has early signs almost impossible to distinguish from those of kennel cough;

Canine herpesvirus, a DNA virus that, like canine adenovirus-2, causes moderate upper respiratory tract infections; and

Pasteurella multocida, a bacterium found in the upper respiratory tract that can contribute to the overall syndrome.

Signs. Although the signs vary depending upon the pathogen or combination of pathogens involved, the first obvious sign is usually moist coughing and the release of sputum. After several days the cough becomes harsh, dry, and almost nonproductive and takes on a hacking, irritating quality, possibly caused by irritation of the vocal mechanism and the early stages of laryngitis. Almost anything will induce the sudden bouts of coughing, including emotional stress, excitement, even drinking water. In some extreme cases a discharge from the nose and eyes is present and may be followed by lethargy, fever, and loss of appetite. These signs begin to resemble the early stages of canine distemper. The cough will persist at its optimum for several weeks and decrease to a low-level cough for possibly one or two months. The signs of kennel cough are persistent, long-lived, and unpleasant for the dog and the humans surrounding him.

Treatment. Limited activity is advised; the dog should be kept warm, comfortable, and free of emotional stress. An environment without cold drafts is beneficial. In some cases antibiotics are recommended along with cough suppressant medications. Various drugs are also available to widen clogged airways, reduce inflammation, or break up mucous secretions within the airway and are prescribed by a veterinarian when appropriate. In extreme situations intravenous administration of fluids becomes necessary.

Vaccination for kennel cough is recommended but is not 100 percent effective in all dogs. Vaccines combining agents for Bordetella bronchiseptica, canine parainfluenza virus, and canine adenovirus-2 offer the best opportunity for protection. However, it is somewhat like vaccinating for the common cold.

A good prevention program must include keeping kennels and areas occupied by dogs meticulously clean and disinfected with various commercial products or with a cholorine bleach solution consisting of 1 part bleach to 32 parts water.

Canine Coronavirus Enteritis

This infectious enteritis can affect dogs of all ages, although young puppies and adult dogs in stress are at the greatest risk. Coronavirus infection can range from insignificant to life-threatening.

Signs. Varied, from mild infections to sudden death. Clinical signs may include loss of appetite, depression, vomiting, diarrhea, and dehydration. The feces may be loose, yellow-orange, and contain strands of blood or mucus. In some cases canine coronavirus enteritis is seen in combination with other pathogens, such as parvovirus.

Treatment. Similar to parvovirus. Veterinary care is required but is supportive rather than curative. Control of vomiting and diarrhea is necessary to prevent extreme fluid loss from the body. In some cases intravenous replacement of fluids is necessary. Vaccine for coronavirus is available but should be given after evaluation by a veterinarian as to its practicality for a specific dog.

von Willebrand's Disease

As the popularity of a breed increases, so do the possibilities for congenital disorders such as von Willebrand's disease (vWD). This "bleeding disease" is similar to hemophilia; it has been reported in more than fifty dog breeds and is on the rise.

Chronic in nature, vWD is characterized by deficiencies in the blood's clotting factors, causing serious medical problems. The severity of the disease varies from dog to dog, with the mildest forms being much more common. Signs and symptoms include hematomas (bruises), nosebleeds, recurring lameness (from blood in the joints), bleeding from the genitalia, and failure of the blood to clot after minor cuts and surgical procedures. Stillborn puppies and early puppy deaths have been attributed to von Willebrand's disease.

To diagnose the disease, a veterinarian takes blood samples and sends them to a laboratory for special testing. Treatment is supportive and includes drug therapies and blood transfusions. Consult a veterinarian about avoiding anything that might cause bleeding, such as medications (aspirin), feeding your dog bones or biscuits, intramuscular injections, closely clipped nails, surgery, internal and external parasites, and potentially abrasive pens or crates.

To reduce the prevalence of von Willebrand's disease in German Shepherds, breeders are urged to have their dogs' blood tested. If any of their dogs are determined to be carriers of the disease, they should be removed from the breeding program.

Internal Parasites

Almost all internal parasites that infect a dog's body are commonly referred to as "worms." They vary in type, size, effect, and danger to the health of the dog. Although internal parasites can do harm to the dog's body, with early detection and treatment, few create permanent or irreparable damage. When treated promptly, the infected dog returns to good health. Depending on the degree of infestation, the condition runs from mild to extremely serious.

Internal parasites are among the most common ailments of dogs and other animals. Almost all puppies have them, and adult dogs get them at one time or another. They must be treated as swiftly as possible by a veterinarian.

All worms have some signs in common that can alert the dog owner to get help for the dog. The early signs include a lethargic manner, inconsistent appetite, diarrhea, and blood in the stool. The signs of heavy infestation are weight loss, bloated stomach, loss of fluid, dry and thinning coat, constant drowsiness, and anemia.

There are many species of internal parasites that infect dogs, but only the most common species are included in this limited segment.

Roundworms (Ascarids)

There is no parasite more common to dogs than roundworms. They are white and resemble spaghetti or earthworms. They are most often seen in the dog's stool or vomitus. The worms range in length from one to seven inches long. The eggs are protected by a hard shell and can live for long periods of time in the soil. The adult worm embeds in the intestinal tract and there deposits its eggs, then passes out of the body through the stool. If the eggs are then ingested by a host, the life cycle is completed and starts again. By eating the eggs in infested soil or fecal matter, the dog becomes infested. Ingestion of infested rodents, birds, and insects also allows entry to a host animal. Ascarids are very commonly found in newborn puppies because of the mother's infection during pregnancy, although the mother need not be infected for puppies to be invaded by these parasites. This happens when the dormant larvae from the mother become active and circulate through the blood system as well as getting into the breast milk. Most puppies are born with roundworms. Adult dogs seldom experience serious illness from ascarids. However, infection can be fatal for heavily infested puppies. All roundworm infestations must be treated quickly. Proper worming and good sanitation are the best preventive methods of control. Consult a veterinarian for diagnosis and treatment.

Children can also be infected with worms by ingesting contaminated soil or feces.

Hookworms (*Ancylostoma caninum*)

Hookworms fasten themselves to the wall of the intestine and draw blood from their host. They range in length from one-fourth to one-half inch long. Dogs acquire these worms from infected soil or feces. Immature worms migrate to the intestine, where they grow into adults. Eggs are passed into the stool in approximately two weeks, thus completing the cycle.

The majority of infections are found in puppies of two to eight weeks of age, with infection from mothers' milk. The infestation can be life-threatening to puppies. Adult dogs are also vulnerable to infection, although not as seriously as puppies. Signs of major hookworm infestation are diarrhea, anemia, noticeable weight loss, and increasing fatigue. Stools become bloody, dark to black in color, and tar-like. Hookworm disease that causes severe anemia is a medical emergency requiring hospitalization and intense veterinary treatment, possibly involving blood transfusions, medication to kill the larvae quickly, and therapies designed to attack migrating larvae remaining within the tissue.

Adults or puppies that recover will probably be carriers because of a small number of arrested larvae and eggs lodged in the tissue. Follow-up treatment is required.

Diagnosis is ascertained by microscopic identification of the eggs in the infected dog's feces. Normal treatment involves orally introduced anthelmintic medications prescribed by a veterinarian. Professional diagnosis and treatment are essential.

Whipworms (*Trichuris vulpis*)

Whipworms are serious parasites and somewhat difficult to detect. They are threadlike, with one end thicker than the other, giving the appearance of a whip. The worms are approximately two to three inches long and live in the large intestine (cecum), where they attach themselves to the inner walls along the tract from the cecum to the colon. Once whipworm eggs are ingested, they develop into larvae and then grow into adult worms in the large intestine. This takes approximately ten weeks, and they remain there for up to sixteen months. During that period the host animal slowly loses blood, with accompanying loss of weight. Diarrhea becomes frequent, with evidence of blood in the stools of heavily infested dogs. Poor health becomes evident.

Diagnosis is made by microscopic examination of the stool. In difficult cases, examinations must be repeated before the eggs can be detected. There are various forms of medication for whipworms, including tablets and intravenous injections, usually administered over a three-month period, with additional stool examinations.

Tapeworm (*Dipylidium caninum*)

Tapeworm is common among dogs. The most frequent sources of infection are fleas, eating infected raw fish, and eating infected uncooked meat or animal parts. Lice can also be a source of tapeworm.

Tapeworms can vary in length from less than one inch to several feet long. Their bodies are segmented and can be found around the anal area, attached to the coat or the anus. Occasionally several segments pass into the stool, but the head always remains to form new links.

Infection by tapeworm can sometimes take a long time to detect. It can begin with digestive upsets, irregular appetite, weight loss, stomach discomfort, and poor coat condition. Diagnosis is made through examination of fecal matter, although this is sometimes ineffective. Detection is more commonly made by observation of segments in the dog's stool, bed, or anal area.

Treatment involves destroying the head within the host's body. Contact with intermediate hosts, such as mice, rats, squirrels, and rabbits, must be avoided. Medications are applied orally or by intravenous injection in several doses over a specified period of time. See a veterinarian for professional diagnosis and treatment.

Heartworms (*Dirofilaria immitis*)

Heartworm disease is a very serious illness for dogs and can be fatal if not treated promptly and properly. Heartworms are large worms that lodge in the right side of the heart and in the pulmonary vessels of the lung. Consequently, the heart has to work much harder to pump blood to the lungs, placing a damaging strain on the entire circulatory system. Eventually the heart weakens and insufficient blood flow affects almost every other vital organ in the body.

The carrier of heartworm disease is the mosquito, which is the transmitter of the parasite during its larval stage. The female heartworm, while in the host dog's body, produces great quantities of moving embryos called microfilaria. Mosquitoes living on the blood of a host dog ingest the microfilaria, which remain in the mosquitoes' bodies for fourteen to twenty-one days and are then transmitted to the body of the next dog the mosquitoes bite. The heartworms enter the next victim's body in their larval stage by the mosquito's injection and then take five to six months to develop into mature worms.

The signs of an infected dog are exhaustion, coughing, loss of weight despite good diet and appetite, and breathing difficulties. Chronic cough brought about by strenuous exercise is the first symptom of a classic case. Death, in the advanced stage, may be brought about by collapse during severe exercise.

Veterinarians are now able to prevent heartworms with routinely prescribed medications for several months prior to the mosquito season and several months afterward. Blood tests prior to administration of this preventive medication are usual.

External Parasites

Fleas, flies, ticks, and lice are the carriers of disease, allergies, and, in some cases, internal parasites. When a dog's body is infected by external parasites, a veterinarian can best determine what the pests are and how to treat them.

The best treatment for internal and external parasites is a good prevention-control attitude. If a dog becomes infested with parasites, it is not enough to provide medical attention. All areas that the dog inhabits must be cleaned thoroughly with soap and water and attacked with a proper pesticide. Disinfect all locations where the dog might have acquired fleas, ticks, or other carriers, and use the strongest solution possible for kennels and doghouses. Clean out the corners of the house where the dog lies around, and disinfect his sheets, blankets, and other equipment. Spraying the house, furniture, carpets, baseboards, floorboards, crevices, and cracks is necessary to prevent reinfestation. Fleas and ticks and their eggs are tenacious and very difficult to eliminate. In some instances, a professional exterminator is necessary.

Fleas

Fleas live off the blood of the host animal. They can drive the host to distraction with the itching they cause and with their constant, irritating bites for the purpose of drawing blood. They cause anemia and often are the carriers of tapeworm. Fleas can also cause typhus, bubonic plague, rabbit fever, and chronic nonspecific dermatitis (sometimes diagnosed as eczema). Additionally, the fleabites often cause inflammation of the skin, hair loss, and, in some cases, allergic reactions to the bite. Flea infestation is a serious matter.

Fleas are small insects, brown or black in color, wingless, and rapid-moving. They live in the coat of the dog they have infested. Fleas can be found in nearly all parts of your dog's body, but they prefer the neck, tail, head, and chest. One variety prefers the ears and their rims. A favorite hiding place is between the dog's toes and under the tail.

The life span of this difficult pest is one year. Its eggs hatch into larval stages, remaining in the environment up to 300 days. The cycle begins anew when the larvae become adults. Treatment involves interrupting the life cycle and killing off the fleas that have already hatched.

Symptoms of flea infestation are frantic scratching and nipping with the front teeth deep into the coat. A flea-ridden dog often chases his tail, rubs his back on the ground, and even whimpers as he scratches. At these moments the fleas are biting into the skin, taking a blood meal, and moving to another location.

Solving the problem of flea infestation involves treating the dog's environment, indoors and outdoors. Spray or dust his sleeping area with flea-killing products. Next, kill the fleas on the dog's body. Give the dog a bath using a safe flea shampoo or dip. Use a flea collar or douse the dog with flea powder or spray until the situation is under control. The daily use of a flea comb will help determine the progress of the treatment.

Apply insecticide once a week for three weeks in the shrubs and grass where your dog spends time. Inside your home spray deep into the crevices and bedding where your pet sleeps. Spray your carpets and get rid of the vacuum cleaner bags after each use. Flea eggs and larvae thrive in such bags.

The most important aspect of flea control is ridding the dog's environment of fleas as well as treating the dog. Doing one without the other is ineffective. Consult a veterinarian and an exterminator.

Ticks

Ticks are parasites classified as *arachnids* (that is, they are related to spiders, mites, etc.), not as insects. Blood loss and anemia are the potential consequences when ticks attach themselves to a dog's body. The greatest danger from tickbites is the transmission of debilitating and life-threatening diseases. Ticks are occasional carriers of Rocky Mountain spotted fever, tropical canine pancytopenia, and Lyme disease (*Lyme borreliosis*). Some dogs become temporarily paralyzed from a tickbite (*tick paralysis*).

The most common ticks feeding on dogs are the brown dog tick (distributed worldwide) and the American dog tick (found throughout North America, but most commonly along the East Coast). Another variety is the deer tick, one of the greatest carriers of Lyme disease (found in the Northeast and Midwest). In California, Lyme disease is transmitted by the western black-legged tick.

Brown dog ticks establish themselves indoors and in kennels (in cracks, bedding, carpeting, and walls). They can infect dogs at all times of the year.

The life cycle of a tick consists of four stages: an egg stage, a six-legged larva stage, an eight-legged nymph stage, and an eight-legged adult stage.

Ticks jump onto dogs outdoors in warm weather and may live up to a year in each stage. If a brown dog tick infestation exists in your house, an exterminator will be needed to remove the ticks. If the grounds surrounding your house are infested, cut and remove tall growths and have an exterminator or gardener spray or dust with an appropriate pesticide.

Care of the infected dog involves removal of the tick by killing it with an alcohol-soaked cotton swab and pulling it off with tweezers (usually a small male tick exists alongside an engorged female). It is potentially harmful to burn a tick off your dog's body with matches or kerosene. Dispose of the tick in a container of alcohol or flush it.

Some ticks may be removed by hand, using your thumb and fore-finger. However, this is not recommended, considering the possibility of transmission to humans of dangerous diseases, such as Rocky Mountain spotted fever and Lyme disease. It is safest to remove ticks with tweezers, forceps, gloves, or a sheet of plastic wrap to avoid contamination of the fingers. A good flea-and-tick dip is an effective means of killing and removing ticks from the dog's body.

Ticks attach themselves to the skin of the dog and feed on its blood. The dog becomes injured by the irritation of tickbites and the loss of blood. When a tick is pulled away from the dog's skin after it has become attached, a small amount of tissue will also be pulled away. This causes a blood smear and sometimes swelling. An antiseptic or antibacterial medication applied topically is important to prevent infection. The effects from some ticks can produce fever, paralysis, and even death. Some tick diseases can be transmitted to humans.

If your dog is bitten by a tick, talk to a veterinarian about transmitted diseases in your region, particularly Lyme disease. Check your dog's body as well as your own frequently for tick infestation.

Mites

Mites are tiny parasites, barely visible to the naked eye. They are classified as *arachnids* (that is, they are related to spiders, ticks, etc.) rather than as insects and cause serious medical problems and torment for dogs.

Whenever your puppy or adult dog keeps pawing at his ears or has an apparent inflammation of the ear, it is safe to suspect an ear mite infection. These common, parasitic organisms are barely visible but do move quite a bit, and can be seen by the trained professional. Ear mites are minute white life forms seen moving through a mixture of ear wax and dried blood. To rid an infected dog, it is essential that they be diagnosed and treated by a veterinarian.

Two other types of mite cause *canine scabies* and *demodectic mange,* which are serious skin conditions also requiring veterinary treatment.

Canine scabies (also known as sarcoptic mange) causes intense itching, hair loss, and skin eruption.

Demodectic manage does not cause itching but is indicated by hair loss around the head and front legs and reddened, scaly skin.

These unsightly and uncomfortable skin diseases must be treated for the sake of the dog and its family. Canine scabies is contagious to humans, but in a very limited form. It can live only three weeks on the human body but will reappear if the dog is not treated. Demodectic mange is a serious ailment for dogs. However, it is not contagious to humans.

Treatment of all mites requires a veterinarian, whose instructions must be carried out faithfully.

CHAPTER TWELVE

Medical Problems Common to the German Shepherd Dog

Sadly, there are several diseases and medical defects that afflict individual German Shepherds that are frequently passed on genetically from generation to generation. The following diseases and medical conditions are presented here as an aid to the prospective puppy buyer and are also offered as important medical information for those who already live with a Shepherd. It is important to note that the medical conditions listed here are not found in German Shepherd Dogs exclusively. However, these are the conditions that are often seen in this breed.

Individual dogs with a predisposition to most of the following diseases and conditions should be excluded from breeding programs and never be mated. Neutering all males and females carrying these illnesses takes them out of the gene pool and prevents them from passing on their respective medical conditions. It is an important consideration when purchasing a German Shepherd puppy.

Canine Panosteitis

Unique to all large breeds, but especially the German Shepherd, canine panosteitis is more commonly called "wandering lameness." It is also referred to as *enostosis* and *eosinophilic panosteitis*. The results of this debilitating ailment are lameness accompanied by pain; it is more commonly seen in young puppies during their rapid-growth stage.

The disease may begin as early as two months of age and as late as five years. In some dogs the lameness wanders from leg to leg and at times is quite painful. The illness may begin suddenly and spontaneously and leave just as quickly.

As a result of the disease, afflicted dogs lose their appetite, run a slightly elevated temperature, become lethargic, and experience pain when touched in the affected areas of the body. X-rays of the legs are the principal means of diagnosis. The cause of the disease is unknown, and in severe cases a dog may experience long-term muscle weakness. No treatment is available, but the disease is self-limiting, with signs often disappearing by the time the patient is two years of age. Mild pain relievers are sometimes prescribed.

Cataracts

Some German Shepherds have a predisposition to developing cataracts. Cataracts are a clouding of the lens of the eye or its surrounding transparent membrane that obstructs light and vision itself. Any spot found on the lens that is opaque, no matter what the size, is considered a cataract. Cataracts can appear as white flecks in the eye or as a milky or bluish white cast to the lens. Dogs of any age can develop them, but the majority are seen in dogs under the age of five years. Cataracts are either hereditary or nonhereditary. It is impossible to tell the difference by examining the lens.

Checking into the history of an individual dog's line can more accurately determine the possibility of hereditary cataracts than a physical examination can. However, as cataracts also develop in dogs as the result of diabetes, it is important to rule out medical problems as a cause.

Dogs past the age of eight years usually have some degree of haziness in the lens. Opaqueness does not necessarily mean that a dog is blind. Some loss of visual acuity is due to the light not having the lens to focus on. A cataract is important only if vision is impaired. Congenital cataracts generally do not progress to blindness. If sight is lost, it can be corrected if the cataract is removed. Cataract surgery is not recommended until visual impairment affects the dog's ability to get around.

Dogs found to be free of hereditary eye disease by a board-certified veterinary ophthalmologist can be registered with the Canine Eye Registration Foundation (CERF). Puppy buyers should ask for a CERF clearance for the sire and dam. In 1974 the Canine Eye Registration Foundation was established. One of its functions is to collect data concerning various inherited canine eye diseases. For further information write to V.M.D.B.–C.E.R.F., South Campus Courts, Building A, Purdue University, West Lafayette, Indiana 47906.

Degenerative Myelopathy

Degenerative Myelopathy is a gradual deterioration of the spinal cord and is frequently associated with the German Shepherd (among other large breeds). Most veterinarians speculate that this debilitating disease is inherited. It begins in the thoracic area of the spine (above the chest area), with signs appearing between the ages of five and seven years. Indicators of this disease include the dog's dragging his hind legs, uneven wearing of back nails, and stumbling. Although there appears to be a general weakness in the hindquarters of the dog's body, one hind leg is usually affected more than the other.

No effective therapy is available for degenerative diseases. Consequently, there is no known cure at this time. However, exercise plays an important role in delaying the progression of the disease. The attending veterinarian must determine the type of exercise that would be most beneficial, its frequency, and its duration. Other treatments might include anti-inflammatory drugs, painkilling medications, and prescribed doses of vitamin B complex and vitamin E.

Elbow Dysplasia

Elbow dysplasia is found in several breeds of dogs, including the German Shepherd, and is thought to be inherited. The condition is caused by a failure of the bones involving the elbows to unite and move properly or by bone fragments within the joint. All aspects of this condition will produce degenerative joint disease over a period of time. Fragments of bones or cartilage in the elbow joint are abrasive, causing severe irritation. This results in pain and impairment of the dog's movement.

The first signs may appear as early as four months of age. Permanent or recurring lameness in the front legs may result. The elbow will be thrown out of place as the dog walks or runs. In this condition a dog will hold its elbow away from the chest.

Diagnosis is by X-ray. Surgical removal of the bone fragments will relieve the pain and discomfort, but since the process is degenerative, it may not be halted.

Prevention is the most important way to deal with elbow dysplasia. Concerned breeders try to eliminate the disease from their line of dogs by maintaining accurate records; they do not mate dysplastic dogs, which are removed from their breeding program.

The Orthopedic Foundation for Animals (OFA) in 1990 established a registry service for dogs free of elbow dysplasia in addition to their registry for dogs free of hip dysplasia. For a specified fee, the OFA's panel of radiologists will review and evaluate properly taken X-rays of dogs before they are used for breeding. If the dog is found to be free of elbow dysplasia, they will certify it by issuing a number and a certificate of passing. Further information can be obtained by writing to the Orthopedic Foundation for Animals, Inc., University of Missouri, Columbia, Missouri 65211.

Gastric Dilation-Volvulus (Bloat)

This life-threatening disease has two primary aspects: *gastric dilation,* the stomach's stretching and swelling rapidly with air or gas as well as fluids so that it cannot expel (bloat), and *volvulus,* the stomach's severely twisting at both ends, which dangerously accelerates the accumulation of gas, cuts off blood circulation, dislocates surrounding organs (especially the spleen), and promotes severe bacterial infection.

Volvulus (severely twisted stomach) interferes with the flow of blood to the heart, the stomach wall, and the spleen. It also impairs the ability to breathe. What is not understood is whether dilation takes place before or after volvulus and whether one causes the other. The most frequent cause of death before or after surgery is the rupture of the stomach and the resultant bacterial infection that enters the bloodstream.

The dogs most likely to develop sudden bloat or gastric dilation-volvulus are the large- and giant-size breeds with deep chests. German Shepherds are one of many deep-chested dogs, such as Great Danes, Saint Bernards, and Irish Setters, that are high on the danger list for this emergency condition that has taken the lives of even smaller breeds.

The clinical signs of bloat or gastric dilation are enlarged or swelled stomach that is painful to the touch, excessive drooling, depression, restlessness, and unproductive attempts to vomit and defecate.

The clinical signs of volvulus are all of the above but with greater intensity, in addition to labored breathing, pale gums (and other mucous membrane tissues), collapse, and unconsciousness.

Treatment involves immediate veterinary care because the disease progresses rapidly, seriously threatening the life of the dog. It consists of taking X-rays (to determine if the stomach has twisted) and expelling the trapped gas and fluids by inserting a tube into the stomach through the mouth, if possible, or by making a direct incision into the abdomen.

If the stomach has twisted, these procedures are ineffective. Surgery is then the only option to decompress the trapped gas, untwist the stomach, and attach it to the abdominal wall or to one of the ribs. If the dog survives, he will require hospitalization involving intravenous fluids and treatment for shock. Reports indicate a mortality rate as high as 60 percent.

Prevention. Although there may be a genetic predisposition to this disease in certain individual dogs, there are preventive measures that should be taken for large dogs.

1. Do not feed dogs one meal a day. Break it into two or three smaller meals.

2. Limit the dog's water intake directly after a meal.

3. Do not allow the dog to exercise vigorously for at least one hour before eating and two hours after eating. A gentle walk after a meal is desirable.

4. Maintain a low- or non-stress environment around the dog, especially while eating. Avoid loud noises, such as rock music during meals.

5. Elevate the dog's food off the floor.

6. Some signs to watch for include pacing, whining, salivating, hacking attempts to vomit, a swollen stomach, restlessness, anxiety, and difficulty breathing. If these signs are present, rush your dog to a vet.

Hip Dysplasia

Canine hip dysplasia is a complex disease characterized by unstable hip joints and in many cases leads to severe crippling and painful movement. Normally, the "ball" at the top of the thighbone (femur) fits tightly into the socket (acetabulum) of the hipbone. Hip dysplasia causes these "ball-and-socket" joints to develop abnormally and only loosely fit together in the socket. It is usually complicated by the added presence of osteoarthritis, a degenerative joint disease.

Unfortunately, this debilitating condition is on the rise in the German Shepherd. It is generally accepted by most authorities that canine hip dysplasia is an inherited condition, even though dogs with no trace of the condition in their line may also produce puppies with hip dysplasia. Some veterinary researchers suspect that puppies with a predisposition for hip dysplasia are seriously affected by accelerated growth, overfeeding, and inappropriate exercise at too early an age.

Signs. This debilitating disease causes lameness with or without pain. Dysplastic dogs are usually born with normal-appearing hips that gradually undergo a progressive structural change. Noticeable signs may appear as early as four months of age. Dysplastic dogs may indicate they are in pain in the hip region, walk with an abnormal or waddling gait, hop when moving quickly, show difficulty trying to stand up, and exhibit a noticeable widening of the hips.

Diagnosis is confirmed by X-ray at twelve months of age, more or less. An X-ray will show the veterinarian the possible presence of degenerative joint disease (osteoarthritis); the shape, contour, and position of the femoral head; and the shape and depth of the acetabulum, the cup-shaped socket in the hipbone. X-ray is essential for an accurate diagnosis.

Treatment. Treatment may consist of surgical or drug therapies or a combination of both. There is no cure for hip dysplasia, but with proper treatment, afflicted dogs can live long and healthy lives within the limitations imposed by the disease.

Mild analgesics, such as enteric-coated aspirin or buffered aspirin, can be used for mild forms of arthritic pain in mild to moderate forms of the disease. Anti-inflammatory drugs (steroids) are given in the more advanced cases in which osteoarthritis is present. Steroids must be used with extreme care and only under a veterinarian's supervision.

Surgery is usually reserved for advanced cases or for those dogs that have not responded to other types of treatment and are in extreme pain. Among the surgical options are *excision arthroplasty* (removal of the ball at the top of the thighbone), *pelvic rotation* (moving the hip socket to an outward direction, providing more room for the ball of the thighbone), and *total hip replacement,* which has proven to be the most effective of surgical therapies.

Prevention is the most important way to deal with hip dysplasia. See Elbow Dysplasia.

Malabsorption Syndrome

This uncommon medical problem occurs more often in the German Shepherd than in other breeds. This disorder diminishes the small intestine's ability to fully absorb nutrients from digested food.

Clinical signs of this disorder are voracious appetite with no weight gain, unusually large stools with a soapy texture (caused by undigested fat, which has a rancid odor). Dogs with malabsorption problems appear undernourished and thin, with dull, dry coats. Diagnosis is difficult and involves fecal smears, X-ray, measurement of breath hydrogen, and possibly a biopsy.

Treatment involves managing the disease rather than curing it. A controlled diet is essential and may or may not require enzyme additives to the ration. Vitamin and mineral supplementation is often prescribed for malabsorption patients.

Pancreatic Atrophy (Pancreatic Exocrine Insufficiency)

This disease is most commonly observed in the German Shepherd because of poorly developed, or premature atrophy of, exocrine tissue, which is essential for digestion. However, it is often a secondary development of a loss of exocrine cells from acute pancreatitis, which is a severe inflammation of the pancreas. The pancreas is a small organ located next to the small intestine. It produces and secretes insulin and digestive enzymes.

The clinical signs of pancreatic exocrine insufficiency are weight loss and chronic, severe diarrhea. The diagnosis involves a blood test. The disease is treated with a controlled diet and medications that add pancreatic enzymes. Dogs can live relatively normal lives with this condition.

Pyotraumatic Dermatitis ("Hot Spots")

This bacterial skin disease is also referred to by veterinarians as "acute moist dermatitis." Everyone who has ever owned a German Shepherd is sure to have seen their dog experience at least one hot spot in its lifetime. A hot spot is a self-induced trauma caused by licking, biting, scratching, or even mutilating a portion of the skin that itches and irritates with almost unbearable intensity. Because of the severity of the unpleasant sensation involved, the dog inflicts painful damage to its own skin.

Signs. Hot spots appear as enlarged, circular bumps on the surface of the skin that painfully exude pus. They can enlarge quickly to one or more inches in diameter, causing unbearable itching. The hair usually sticks to the area around the sore, forming a hardened scab. Some hair loss is inevitable.

Hot spots can develop as quickly as two hours after the first indications but usually appear overnight. These painful lesions can turn up just about anywhere on a dog's body but are most often seen along the lower back and thighs. They occur just before shedding begins or during warm, humid weather when dead hair is trapped next to the skin, causing abrasive rubbing and itching. Dogs with double coats are especially vulnerable. Other important causes are flea infestation, flea allergy dermatitis, ear infections, impacted or infected anal glands, and various other forms of skin irritation.

Treatment. Clip the hair surrounding the hot spot and gently clean the inflamed area with a surgical soap such as Betadine, Oxydex, or diluted hydrogen peroxide two to three times a day. The wound must be kept clean and dry. Topical antibiotics help to reduce the irritation.

Effective nonprescription medications that soothe and heal hot spots are Sulfodene medication and Sulfodene shampoo. These are the only nonprescription hot spot treatments approved by the FDA and are recommended by many veterinarians.

If the dog continues to harm itself by licking and biting at the area, a veterinarian may recommend an *Elizabethan collar*, which is a rolled sheet of cardboard wrapped around the dog's neck that prevents it from getting at the wound. See a veterinarian if your Shepherd develops hot spots.

Hot spots are common to German Shepherds, among many other breeds, and should have little or no bearing on decisions involving breeding or buying such dogs.

Subvalvular Aortic Stenosis (SAS)

This uncommon condition is inherited and is present at birth, occurring most often in larger dog breeds, such as the German Shepherd. It is a cardiac defect that involves an abnormal narrowing or constriction of the connection between the left ventricle of the heart and the aorta. The condition ranges from mild to severe. There are three forms of aortic stenosis: supravalvular, valvular, and subvalvular.

Subvalvular aortic stenosis, the most common of the three types, limits blood flow from the left ventricle of the heart, causing it to work harder to provide the necessary blood circulation required by the body. The disorder is caused by one or more circular formations of fibrous, scar-like tissue beneath the aortic valve. Although the heart compensates for this abnormality, some affected dogs exhibit an intolerance for exercise. Such dogs will struggle and collapse if pushed into strenuous physical activity. Some affected dogs show few or no signs at all. Congestive heart failure and sudden death in the first three years of life are distinct possibilities in severe cases of SAS.

Suspicion of this condition during a routine veterinary examination of a puppy or young dog is the first phase of diagnosis. The vet will detect a heart murmur during the systolic (contraction) phase of the heartbeat by listening with a stethoscope. The diagnosis is confirmed by X-ray, electrocardiogram, or echocardiogram (determining velocity of blood flow), or by measurements of blood pressure within the stricture taken with an intravenous catheter.

Both mild and severe cases of SAS are treated medically as any other heart patient, with preventive measures involving diet and correction of body chemistry. Treatment of choice for severe cases of SAS is open-heart surgery in an attempt to remove the fibrous tissue causing the constriction.

CHAPTER THIRTEEN

Home Medical Care

Get a Vet

When your dog is sick, it's hard to think of all things bright and beautiful. Whether a dog needs emergency treatment, preventive medicine, or home medical care, pet owners will sooner or later need a veterinarian. A puppy should get a medical examination as the first order of business, and that requires selecting a vet even before selecting a dog. Ideally, the new puppy should be examined by his veterinarian before going home for the first time. If you already have a vet, you will be able to do this and know exactly whom to call in the event of an injury or an emergency, when saving time means saving life.

If you are about to become a dog owner for the first time, you can find doctors of veterinary medicine in the Yellow Pages under "Veterinarians" or "Animal Hospitals." You can also call your local veterinary medical society for referrals.

Most owners accept the recommendation of their dog's breeder or one from their friends. It is important, however, to look for a vet who is close to your home. When considering a veterinarian for your Shepherd, ask about his or her working hours and whether he or she offers emergency care after hours. If not, inquire as to the location of the nearest after-hours emergency care center.

It is important that your first visit be a pleasant one for both you and your puppy. Your vet should want to establish a good working relationship, and you must have full confidence in his or her ability.

Home Medical Kit

It is wise to assemble a home medical kit for simple medical care and emergency first aid. Clearly label your medical supplies and keep them in a closed container. A tackle box makes an ideal first aid kit. It should contain your veterinarian's name, address, phone number, and a current list of medications given to your dog.

Medical Tools

scissors
> straight-edged for cutting bandages, blunt-tipped for cutting hair away from wounds

tweezers
> to remove small objects

forceps
> a surgeon's tool with a locking clamp for grasping, compressing, and pulling

pen light

rectal thermometer

Materials

sterile gauze bandage
> rolled strips 1, 2, and 3 inches wide

large and small gauze pads
> dressings to place over a wound or serve as a compress 3" by 3" or 4" by 4"

cotton balls
> for wiping wounds, for applying ointments, etc.

cotton applicators or swabs
> for applying medications, cleaning wounds, etc.

adhesive tape
> to hold bandages in place

tongue depressors
> to hold mouth open, for makeshift splints

mineral oil
   lubricant
instant cold pack
   to reduce body temperature
instant heat pack
   to provide warmth to the body when necessary

Medicines
hydrogen peroxide, 3 percent solution
   for cleaning cuts and wounds
Bacitracin
   antiseptic, antibacterial skin ointment for cuts, wounds, and
   burns
antiseptic powder or spray
   for cuts, wounds, or burns difficult to reach or pain-sensitive
eye ointment
   the only antiseptic appropriate for eyes
saline eye wash
   to flush the eyes of debris
styptic powder or other form of coagulant
   to stop bleeding
syrup of ipecac
   to induce vomiting; other products for this purpose are hydrogen
   peroxide, salt and water paste, mustard powder paste, etc.
Kaopectate
   to stop diarrhea
liquid antacid or **Pepto-Bismol**
   for digestive upset
activated charcoal
   for absorbing toxic substances in the stomach

Taking Your Dog's Temperature

One of the most significant indications of illness is an abnormal temperature reading, and every dog owner should know how to get a reading. A rectal thermometer from any pharmacy will do, although you can get special ones for dogs from a pet supply store or mail-order catalog.

By necessity, all dog temperature readings must be taken rectally. Shake the thermometer down below 99°F. Allow the dog to stand or place him on his side and lift his tail. Smear the tip of the thermometer (the bulb-shaped end) with petroleum jelly. Insert the thermometer into the dog's anus. If the dog is large, the thermometer should be inserted to approximately half its length. Smaller dogs require about one-inch insertion. Leave the thermometer inside for two to three minutes. Do not allow the dog to move while the thermometer is in his body. Most dogs will hold still for this procedure if petted and spoken to in a soft, comforting tone of voice. Do not allow the dog to sit until the thermometer has been removed.

Remove the thermometer and take the reading. The average reading for a normal dog is approximately 102°F. This indicates no fever. Large dogs will run a slightly lower normal temperature, around 99.5°F. Many veterinarians consider fever to start at a reading of 102.6°F. Record the dog's temperature every time it is taken so that it can be given to your vet on request. If the dog is recovering from a serious illness, a complete record of the daily temperature is invaluable for the dog's doctor.

Administering Medication

Pills and tablets. First, tilt the dog's head back. To open his mouth, insert a finger behind the canine teeth. Take the pill between your thumb and index finger and place the pill on the tongue, as far back as possible. Close the dog's mouth and gently stroke his throat to make him swallow. If the dog will not allow you to open his mouth, try putting the pill in a piece of cheese or canned dog food to disguise it. The only way to be certain the dog has ingested his medication is to make sure he has eaten all his food. Coating the pill or tablet with oil or butter is also useful.

Liquid medicine. Purchase a plastic syringe from your pharmacist or veterinarian to make this chore easier. Eyedroppers and spoons can also be used. Fill the syringe or eyedropper with the correct dose of medication. (Do not attach a needle to the syringe.) Tilt the dog's head at a 45-degree angle and place the syringe between the molars and the cheek. Holding the cheek closed with your fingers, gently squeeze in the liquid. Sometimes liquids can be mixed into food, but be certain only a small amount of food is used, to ensure that the dog gets all the medication.

Eye medication. When applying eye medication, pull down the lower lid and apply ointment to the inner surface of the eyelid with an applicator. *Do not* touch the eye with the end of the applicator or try to apply the medication into the middle of the eye. This could cause the dog to jerk and result in serious eye injury. Eye drops can be applied directly to the eyeball. Rub the eyelid gently to disperse the medicine. When medicating the eye, never use medications that are outdated or not labeled specifically for ophthalmologic use.

Eye problems should never be neglected with a wait-and-see attitude. If you are treating your dog's eye at home and there is no improvement within twenty-four hours, see a veterinarian immediately. Blindness or severe complications could be the result of waiting too long.

CHAPTER FOURTEEN

The Most-Asked Questions about the German Shepherd Dog

1. Do German Shepherds shed?

Yes. The breed has a double coat, which means it consists of a hard outer coat and a softer, insulating undercoat. The undercoat sheds in the spring and in warm weather. After the initial puppy coat changes to an adult coat, males shed once a year and unspayed females shed twice a year, usually after a heat (estrus). Dogs that spend more time outdoors in cool climates maintain their coats longer. Dogs living indoors shed considerably more. Long hours spent under artificial lighting is the suspected cause.

Continual shedding can be kept to a minimum with weekly or daily brushing all year long. Once the coat begins its full, seasonal shed, a warm bath with vigorous brushing afterward speeds the process along. The removal of dead hair is important to ease the itching that a loose coat causes. This is essential to protect against self-mutilation and *hot spots* (see Chapter Twelve, "Medical Problems Common to the German Shepherd Dog"). The sooner the dead hair is brushed out, the quicker the natural process of regrowth will begin. A commercial vacuum cleaner is well worth the investment for your home, and a shedding coat is well worth the trouble for the benefit of sharing your home with a German Shepherd.

2. If I want my German Shepherd to protect me, isn't it best not to let him make friends with people?

When is my puppy an adult?

Absolutely not. An unsocialized German Shepherd becomes overprotective and territorial and possibly dangerous. All the best protection dogs are encouraged to be friendly with all people. Protecting you is just a job enhanced by the bond between the dog and your family; otherwise, the dog becomes an unpredictable bomb waiting to go off.

3. When is my puppy an adult?

Shepherds generally mature after the second year. However, some Shepherd lines mature quicker while others may take as long as two to three years. Many adult Shepherds maintain a playful puppy personality throughout their entire life.

4. Are so-called giant German Shepherds or occasional long-haired German Shepherds more intelligent or more valuable in any way?

No. As a matter of fact, oversized German Shepherds can be clumsy in the performance of their work and have the added health problems associated with giant breeds. Although these Shepherds make excellent pets and are responsive to training, there is no particular advantage to them.

Long-coated dogs show up frequently in a breed that is normally short-coated because of a recessive gene. Such dogs are not qualified to enter conformation dog shows, because they do not represent their breed standard. Of course, this does not detract from their training or working abilities.

Long-coated and oversized Shepherds should not be considered rare or of greater value. Whether they are puppies or adults, their cost should not be greater than that of a German Shepherd Dog that truly represents its breed according to its breed standard.

5. Can I show my white German Shepherd?

Not in American Kennel Club conformation shows. White is considered a disqualifying color. However, white Shepherds may be entered in AKC performance tests.

6. My one-year-old German Shepherd is smart and obedient but is distracted by everything. When will he grow up and pay attention to me?

Try looking at your pup as alert and interested in his surroundings—a desirable trait in a protection dog. A German Shepherd matures after two years of age (in some dogs, after two to three years). Continue to train with patience and remember that he is just a baby. Enjoy his youth.

7. Should I bike or road-work my puppy for exercise?

No puppy under a year old should receive this strenuous form of exercise. Free play and walks are recommended for dogs under one year of age, until their bones are formed and hard. Young dogs should avoid jogging or running on hard surfaces because doing so can cause serious physical damage. Roadwork should start slowly and must be carefully monitored. Although retrieving games are fun and healthy, jumping and twisting exercises for young pups, such as chasing a Frisbee, can be detrimental to bones and joints still forming. A Shepherd puppy will run or play to please you beyond what may be safe. Steady, gradually increased exercise builds strong muscles to support joints and to increase stamina.

8. How often should I bathe my German Shepherd Dog?

If your dog is dirty, he needs a bath. A regularly brushed dog with a proper coat needs less frequent bathing. Any evidence of dirt or parasites on the skin indicates that the dog needs a bath. Dirty skin is itchy and unpleasant for your dog and for you. If he is a house dog, you will not appreciate doggie BO. A sensible formula is to bathe your dog once a month and brush him daily. Ask your veterinarian or professional groomer for the correct shampoo for your dog's coat type and texture.

9. How long do German Shepherds live?

Life expectancy of a German Shepherd is nine to twelve years, with many breed lines living much longer.

10. Do I have to obedience-train my German Shepherd Dog?

Definitely. Shepherds are much too strong-willed to be allowed to have things their own way. Training a Shepherd is very satisfying because of their intelligence and willingness to please.

11. Should I show my dog?

If the dog has show potential and is physically sound, and if you have the time and money to invest, why not? Consult your breeder or professional handler. Study the standard for the breed and don't go into showing to make money from your dog. You won't. It should be a way to have fun and show pride in your beautiful friend.

12. Should I breed my German Shepherd Dog?

Only if you are considering it to improve the breed and have a Shepherd that is physically sound and has been proved to be a correct type and temperament against others of his breed in competition. Be willing to follow up on all puppies you have bred.

13. Should I spay or neuter my Shepherd?

If you are not showing in conformation or planning to breed your dog, you should absolutely spay or neuter your dog. It is easier on you and the dog emotionally and physically and will help prevent certain health problems. Consult your veterinarian for details. Spay-

If you get a second dog, be prepared to double the time you spend grooming, exercising, and giving individual attention to both pets.

ing or neutering will not make your dog fat or lazy and does not change his or her personality.

14. Doesn't a Shepherd need a big yard? I live in an apartment and don't think it would be fair to own one.

It would be fair if you were willing to train the dog and provide adequate exercise. Shepherds make excellent apartment dwellers.

15. Should I get another German Shepherd to keep my current one company?

Yes and no. Your Shepherd will adore a new companion. They will both give you years of pleasure and they will thoroughly enjoy being with each other. However, if you get a second dog, it should be for you. Be prepared to spend double the time on grooming and exercise as well as double the cost for veterinary care, vaccinations, food, and other unexpected expenses. Most important, be willing to double the time you devote to giving the individual attention every dog needs and deserves.

16. Are Shepherds good with children?

Yes. They are among the best of all breeds with children. But as with any breed, good sense should be used when it comes to child-dog interaction. Puppies and adult dogs should not be left unsupervised with young children. Little puppies will not be able to handle the roughness of ear and tail pulling and could be dropped and injured. The adult dog, however gentle, could accidentally bump and knock down a small child unintentionally.

17. Should I own a German Shepherd Dog?

Yes. If you want the total dog, this is the breed for you. The Shepherd is a loving pet and companion and great family dog, particularly because of their fondness for children. At the same time, Shepherds protect all members of their family as well as guard their home. The security a Shepherd provides gives peace of mind to all those who live with one. German Shepherds are intelligent, athletic, and beautiful.

APPENDIX

◆ ◆

Guide Dog Schools

From *A Guide to Guide Dog Schools*, by Ed and Toni Eames, second edition, copyright © 1994 (self-published), with permission.

The three breeds most commonly used [as Guide Dogs] are Labrador Retrievers, Golden Retrievers, and German Shepherd Dogs. Most schools train both male and female dogs, all of whom are neutered. Schools obtain their dogs by breeding their own or through purchase or donation. From this stock the schools carefully select the animals they believe can be trained to make the best guides.

At about the age of two months, puppies selected for future guide dog training are placed with families, known as puppy raisers or puppy walkers. These invaluable volunteers are expected to introduce the puppies to a wide variety of experiences, such as interaction with other animals, children and exposure to the noise and confusion of family living. The puppies learn to travel in cars and accompany their raisers in public places as much as possible. In addition these devoted volunteers housebreak the puppies and teach them basic manners. Above all, the puppy raisers provide the tender loving care necessary for proper socialization.

When the young dogs are approximately 14 to 18 months of age, their serious training starts back at the school. Professional instructors who have gone through a thorough apprenticeship program work with the dogs for the next three to six months preparing them for their future work as guides.

Becoming a guide dog is not easy. A guide dog should be physically healthy, intelligent, responsive and friendly. A guide dog should not be fearful, aggressive or hyperactive. From earliest puppyhood dogs are continuously evaluated for their future careers. During the year with the puppy raisers, some dogs show indications they would not be good guides and are rejected for further training. The young dogs brought back to the school are further tested for suitable temperaments before going on for formal training. Throughout the training period, any dog deemed unsuitable is disqualified. The schools usually have more dogs available than the actual number of students coming in for training, so further selection takes place during the matching process.

According to Ed and Toni Eames, "Only half the dogs bred or donated as future guides actually graduate. With a current total of 1,300 graduating, this means a minimum of 1,300 dogs are released as pets."

It is their suggestion that those desiring a German Shepherd be aware of Guide Dog schools as a source of well-bred puppies and adult dogs that for one reason or another were not suited for that highly specialized work. At this writing there are fourteen American and two Canadian programs that serve as a possible source for an available dog.

A List of Guide Dog Schools

UNITED STATES
Eye Dog Foundation of Arizona (Eye Dog)
8252 South 15th Avenue
Phoenix, AZ 85041
602-276-0051

(administrative office)
512 North Larchmont Boulevard
Los Angeles, CA 90004

Fidelco Guide Dog Foundation Inc. (Fidelco)
P.O. Box 142
Bloomfield, CT 06002
203-243-5200
203-243-7215 (fax)

Freedom Guide Dogs (Freedom)
1210 Hardscrabble Road
Cassville, NY 13318
315-822-5132

Guide Dogs of America (GDA)
13445 Glenoaks Boulevard
Sylmar, CA 91342
818-362-5834
818-362-6870 (fax)

Guide Dogs for the Blind, Inc. (Guide Dogs)
P.O. Box 151200
San Rafael, CA 94915-1200
415-499-4000
800-295-4050
415-499-4035 (fax)

Guide Dogs of the Desert, Inc. (GDD)
P.O. Box 1692
Palm Springs, CA 92263
619-329-6257
619-329-2127 (fax)

Guide Dog Foundation for the Blind, Inc. (The Foundation)
371 East Jericho Turnpike
Smithtown, NY 11787-2976
516-265-2121 (N.Y. State)
800-548-4337 (outside N.Y. State)
516-361-5192 (fax)
516-366-4462 (computer bulletin board)

Guiding Eyes for the Blind, Inc. (GEB)
611 Granite Springs Road
Yorktown Heights, NY 10598
914-245-4024
800-942-0149
914-245-1609 (fax)

Kansas Specialty Dog Service (KSDS)
P.O. Box 216, Highway 36
Washington, KS 66968
913-325-2256
913-325-2258 (fax)

Leader Dogs for the Blind (Leader)
1039 South Rochester Road
P.O. Box 5000
Rochester, MI 48307
810-651-9011
810-651-5812 (fax)

Pilot Dogs Inc. (Pilot)
625 West Town Street
Columbus, OH 43215
614-221-6367
614-221-1577 (fax)

The Seeing Eye, Inc. (Seeing Eye)
P.O. Box 375
Morristown, NJ 07963-0375
800-539-4425

Southeastern Guide Dogs Inc. (Southeastern)
4210 77th Street, East
Palmetto, FL 34221
813-729-5665
813-729-6646 (fax)

Upstate Guide Dog Association, Inc. (Upstate)
P.O. Box 165
Hamlin, NY 14464
716-964-8815

CANADA
Canadian Guide Dogs for the Blind (CGDG)
P.O. Box 280
4120 Rideau Valley Drive North
Manotick, Ontario
Canada K4M 1A3
613-692-7777
613-692-0650 (fax)

Canine Vision Canada
P.O. Box 907
152 Wilson Street
Oakville, Ontario
Canada L6K 3H2

La Fondation Mira Inc. (Mira)
1820 Rang Nord-Ouest
Sainte-Madeleine QC
Canada J0H 1S2
514-875-6668
514-795-3789 (fax)

PHOTOGRAPH

CREDITS

All photographs are by Barbara von Hoffmann except where indicated. Among the dogs (and persons) appearing in the photographs are:

Cover: Adult, Alorah vom Hochland, Puppy, Elladryll vom Hochland, Owner: Glenn McIntosh.

Page 7: Tosh. Owner: Neil Drury, Jr.

Page 25: TNC's Montana Mike, SchH 1 FH. Owners: Tom and Christine Hendrickson.

Page 34: Dozer vom Schneider, SchH II, OFA. Trainer: Douglas Calhoun.

Page 40: Jeana vom Hochland (left) and Alorah vom Hochland (right). Owner: Glenn McIntosh.

Page 47: Rommel II vom Haus Barwig. Owner: Barbara von Hoffmann.

Page 62: Rommel II vom Haus Barwig. Owner: Barbara von Hoffmann.

Page 79: Tosh. Owner: Neil Drury, Jr.

Page 154: Tosh. Owner: Neil Drury, Jr.

Page 212: V Mandie aus der Hauffstrasse, SchH II, KKL 1a OFA (right) and V Valant vom BierstaderHof Sch IPO III, FH, KKL 1a, OFA. Owner: Susan Barwig.

Index